Change Your Life in 30 Days

A Guide to Personal Transformation

Trevor Atkinson

Copyright © 2024

All rights reserved.

All rights reserved. No part of this publication may be reproduced, distributed, or transmitted in any form or by any means, including photocopying, recording, or other electronic or mechanical methods, without the author's prior written permission, except in the case of brief quotations embodied in critical reviews and certain other non-commercial uses permitted by copyright law. For permission requests, please get in touch with the author.

Contents

Dedication i

Acknowledgments ii

About the Author iv

Introduction 4

    Welcome & Overview 4

    Understanding the Importance of behavioural Change 6

    Setting the Stage for the 30-Day Transformation Journey 8

Part 1 Understanding behavioural Patterns 10

Chapter 1 *Becoming Aware of Our behavioural Patterns: A Prelude to Transformation* 11

    Exploring the Concept of behaviour and Its Impact on Our Lives: A Profound Journey into Self-Understanding 13

    The Power of Self-Reflection and Introspection 14

    Practical Exercises to Increase Self-Awareness: Navigating the Path to Transformation 19

Chapter 2 *Uncovering Psychological Triggers - Navigating the Depths of Influence* 27

    Understanding the Psychology Behind Triggers and Their Influence: Decoding the Patterns of Emotional Response 33

    Identifying Common Triggers and Their Effects on behaviour: Decoding the Blueprint of Emotional Responses 39

    Techniques for Managing and Overcoming Triggers: A Journey to Emotional Mastery 44

Chapter 3 *The Influence of Childhood on Our Perception - Nurturing Seeds, Shaping Horizons* 52

    Examining the Role of Childhood Experiences: Seeds of Our Worldview 52

    Recognizing the Impact of Early Experiences: The Imprint on Beliefs and behaviours 53

    Healing and Reframing Past Narratives: A Journey to Positive Change 54

Chapter 4 *The Connection between Identity and Decision Making* 69

    Exploring the Relationship between Identity and Decision-Making Processes: The Tapestry of Self in Choices 69

    Identifying Limiting Beliefs and Their Effect on Choices: Unveiling the Chains that Bind 73

    Cultivating a Positive and Empowering Self-Identity: The Art of Self-Transformation 78

Part 2 Strategies and Tools for Behavioural Change 84

Chapter 5 *Setting Powerful Intentions* 87

    Understanding the Importance of Clear Intentions in Driving Change 88

    Crafting Meaningful and Achievable Goals: The Art of Intentional Living 95

    Techniques for Setting Intentions Effectively: A Blueprint for Intentional Living 101

Chapter 6 *Building New Habits* 109

The Science of Habit Formation and Its Impact on behaviour: Unraveling the Neural Tapestry of Routine 109

Strategies for Breaking Old Habits: Liberation from Unwanted Routines 117

Creating Supportive Environments for Habit Development: Nurturing the Soil for Growth... 123

Chapter 7 *Managing Resistance and Overcoming Obstacles* 129

Recognizing and Addressing Resistance to Change: Illuminating the Shadows of Transformation 130

Strategies for Addressing Resistance: A Compass for Change 133

Cultivating Resilience and Perseverance in the Face of Challenges: The Art of Triumph over Adversity..................... 140

Chapter 8 *Mindset Shifts for Transformation: A Journey into the Power of Perspective* 146

The Role of Mindset in behavioural Change: Unlocking the Gateway to Transformation 146

Harnessing the Power of Positive Thinking and Self-Belief: Illuminating the Path to Transformation................................ 149

Techniques for Cultivating Positive Thinking: A Radiant Mindset 157

Part 3 The 30-Day Diary - A Journey Within............................ 160

Chapter 9 *Preparing for Your Transformation Journey* 161

Setting the Stage for the 30-Day Diary: A Prelude to Transformation 164

Guidelines for Documenting Progress and Experiences: Navigating the Tapestry of Transformation 169

Cultivating a Supportive Mindset for the Journey Ahead: Nurturing the Seeds of Transformation 175

Chapter 10-39 *Embarking on the Daily Journey: A Preview of Chapters 10-39* 182

Chapter 40 *Embracing Transformation: A Prelude to Chapter 40* 244

Wrapping Up the 30-Day Transformation Journey: A Tapestry of Growth 245

Reflecting on Progress and Lessons Learned: The Mirrors of Transformation 246

Celebrating Achievements and Embracing a Transformed Future: A Symphony of Triumph 248

Conclusion 250

Recap of Key Takeaways: 250

Encouragement for Continued Growth: 250

Final Thoughts on the Power of behavioural Change: 251

Dedication

This book is dedicated with love, to my wife Georgie.

Acknowledgments

In the creation of this self-help guide, I find myself humbled and deeply grateful for the multitude of individuals who have contributed to its realization. Foremost among them are the clients, both past and present, who have entrusted me with the privilege of being part of their transformative journeys.

To those individuals who have graciously allowed me into the sacred space of their personal growth, thank you for the honour. Your courage, resilience, and commitment to change have not only shaped the content of this book but have left an indelible mark on my understanding of the human spirit.

I extend my sincere appreciation to each client who, through their stories, struggles, and triumphs, has enriched the narrative within these pages. Your willingness to embrace change, to confront challenges, and to seek growth has been the driving force behind the insights shared in this guide.

This book stands as a collective tribute to the countless individuals who have inspired me with their vulnerability and dedication to self-discovery. Your stories have been the fuel that propelled me to explore the depths of personal development and to distill practical lessons for the benefit of all.

To all my clients, past and present, thank you for the privilege of being part of your transformative journey. May the wisdom shared within these pages be a reflection of the strength, courage, and resilience that you have demonstrated on your paths to self-discovery.

With heartfelt gratitude,

Trev February '24

About the Author

Trev, an Honors degree Psychologist, Hypnotherapist and Master Practitioner of Neuro Linguistic Programming, is a seasoned Mind coach with over a decade of experience. He empowers individuals to overcome obstacles and propel their lives forward, specializing in guiding transformative journeys. Having studied across Europe, North America, and Asia, Trev's expertise transcends borders. His counseling expertise extends to fostering healthy connections, aiding those grappling with personal challenges, and nurturing emotional well-being. Trev's approach encompasses understanding and overcoming life's stressors, ensuring mental resilience. In his practice, he skillfully navigates clients through relational intricacies, empowering them to embark on meaningful self-discovery and fostering positive behavioral shifts.

Introduction: How to use this book

Embarking on the transformative odyssey outlined in this book requires a strategic and purposeful approach. Unlike a novel, this guide is a roadmap to self-discovery and behavioural change. To maximize its impact, consider approaching this guide as a dynamic companion, an active participant in your transformational process. Navigate its pages deliberately, engage with the content purposefully, and let the journey unfold in a way that best serves your unique path to personal growth. Remember, this is not just a book; it's a toolkit for shaping the life you aspire to live.

Part 1: Understanding Behavioural Patterns

Read: Dive into the exploration of behavioural science, unravelling the intricacies of your triggers and understanding why certain patterns persist.

Reflect: Pause after each section, contemplating your own responses, self-sabotage tendencies, and unmet potentials.

Reveal: Delve into the reasons behind your actions, unveiling the layers of your behaviour to lay the groundwork for transformation.

Part 2: Strategies and Tools for Behavioural Change

Apply: Utilize the tools, resources, and strategies presented in Part 2. Experiment with various examples and tips tailored to your uniqueness.

Test: Embrace the understanding that not every method works for everyone. Test different approaches, keeping what works and discarding what doesn't.

Adjust: Recognize that the journey to behavioural change is not instantaneous. Allow time for adjustment, understanding that progress is gradual and requires patience.

Part 3: 30-Day Diary on Changing Your Life

Start: Choose a commencement day that suits you, whether it's the first of the month or a Monday. Research indicates increased success rates when starting on these days.

Track: Use the provided pages to meticulously track successes and setbacks, offering insights into your transformational journey.

Reflect: Engage in the Start, Stop, Continue method at the end of Part 3. Assess what elements to introduce, remove, and sustain, fostering continuous growth.

Celebrate: Recognize and celebrate your transformation, acknowledging the progress made and envisioning a future shaped by intentional choices.

Overall Approach:

Read, Reflect, Reveal: Navigate the content of Part 1 with a reflective mindset, unravelling the complexities of your behaviour.

Apply, Test, Adjust: Implement the diverse strategies in Part 2, testing and adjusting to find what resonates with your unique self.

Start, Track, Reflect, Celebrate: Embark on the 30-day journey in Part 3, starting on a day of significance, tracking your progress, reflecting on your transformation, and celebrating the positive changes achieved.

This user's guide encourages a thoughtful and iterative approach to personal transformation, emphasizing self-awareness, adaptability, and the celebration of progress along the way.

Introduction

Welcome & Overview

Welcome to "Change Your Life in 30 Days: A Guide to Personal Transformation." This book is your passport to a journey of self-discovery and empowerment, where each page is a stepping stone toward a more fulfilled and purposeful life. In the hustle and bustle of our daily routines, we often find ourselves caught in behavioural patterns that may not serve our greater well-being. The key to unlocking personal growth lies in understanding these patterns, unraveling the psychological triggers that influence our decisions, and forging a path towards positive change.

This guide begins with an exploration of self-awareness in Part 1, encouraging you to delve into the intricacies of your behavioural patterns and the psychological triggers that shape your responses. We deep dive into the profound impact of childhood experiences on your perceptions and beliefs, offering tools to heal and reframe past narratives.

In Part 2, we equip you with a toolbox of strategies for meaningful behavioural change. Learn the art of setting powerful intentions and crafting achievable goals, explore the science behind habit formation, and discover how to navigate resistance and overcome obstacles. This section also delves into the transformative power of mindset shifts, helping you cultivate a growth-oriented perspective.

The heart of the book lies in Part 3, where you embark on a 30-day transformation journey with a dedicated diary. Each day is an opportunity for self-reflection, gratitude, and action, guiding you through prompts and providing space for personal notes. The journey culminates in a chapter of reflection and celebration, acknowledging your progress and setting the stage for a future filled with purpose and positive change.

As you embark on this transformative adventure, remember that change is not only possible but within your grasp. This book is your companion, offering insights, tools, and encouragement as you rewrite the script of your life. Embrace the power of behavioural change, and let the next 30 days be the beginning of a lifelong journey towards a happier, more authentic version of yourself.

Congratulations on taking the first step!

Understanding the Importance of behavioural Change

Behavioural change is not merely a personal choice; it is the cornerstone of personal development and a gateway to a more fulfilling and purpose-driven life. At its core, behavioural change is about breaking free from autopilot responses and consciously choosing actions that align with our aspirations. The importance of embracing behavioural change transcends individual well-being; it ripples through relationships, work, and overall life satisfaction.

Firstly, behavioural change is essential for unlocking our true potential. Often, we unknowingly adhere to patterns and habits that limit our growth. By becoming aware of these patterns and making intentional choices, we pave the way for self-discovery and personal evolution. This process empowers us to transcend self-imposed limitations, fostering a sense of agency over our lives.

Secondly, behavioural change plays a pivotal role in enhancing the quality of our relationships. As we become more attuned to our responses and triggers, we develop a heightened empathy and understanding of others. This newfound awareness fosters healthier communication, reduces conflicts, and strengthens connections. By working on ourselves, we contribute positively to the dynamics of the communities we engage in.

Moreover, behavioural change is instrumental in navigating life's challenges. Resilience is cultivated through the ability to adapt and respond constructively to setbacks. By understanding and altering our behavioural responses, we equip ourselves with the tools needed to confront obstacles with grace and determination. This adaptability not only eases the journey through adversity but also fosters personal growth in the face of challenges.

The impact of behavioural change extends to our overall well-being, encompassing physical health, mental resilience, and emotional balance. Breaking unhealthy habits and cultivating positive ones positively influences our energy levels, stress management, and emotional intelligence. In essence, it lays the groundwork for a holistic and harmonious life.

The importance of behavioural change lies in its transformative potential. It is the key to unlocking a life of purpose, fulfillment, and resilience. As you embark on this 30-day journey of personal transformation, remember that each intentional shift in behaviour brings you closer to the vibrant, empowered version of yourself you aspire to become. Embrace change as a constant companion on your journey toward a brighter, more authentic future.

Setting the Stage for the 30-Day Transformation Journey

Welcome to the pivotal moment where you stand at the threshold of a transformative adventure, ready to embark on a 30-day journey of self-discovery and positive change. Before we delve into the practical steps and daily reflections, it's crucial to set the stage for this transformative experience.

First and foremost, take a moment to acknowledge your decision to embark on this journey. Recognize the courage it takes to commit to personal growth and the power you hold to shape your own destiny. Embrace the idea that change is not only possible but entirely within your grasp. The next 30 days are an opportunity to cultivate habits that align with your aspirations and steer your life toward greater fulfillment.

Consider dedicating a space for reflection, whether it's a quiet corner in your home or a cozy spot in nature. This will be your sanctuary for introspection, goal setting, and envisioning the life you wish to create. A designated space fosters a sense of mindfulness, signaling to your subconscious mind that this time is sacred and dedicated to your personal transformation.

As you prepare for the journey ahead, adopt an attitude of openness and curiosity. Embrace the unknown and view each day as a canvas waiting for your intentional strokes. Allow yourself to be present in each moment, appreciating the opportunities for growth and learning that will undoubtedly arise.

Establish a routine that accommodates the daily commitments of the 30-day diary. Whether it's dedicating a few moments in the morning or evening, consistency is key. By integrating these reflections into your daily life, you create a rhythm that enhances the impact of the transformative process.

Finally, cultivate a mindset of self-compassion. Understand that change is a gradual and sometimes challenging process. Be kind to yourself on this journey, celebrating victories, no matter how small, and learning from moments of difficulty. Remember, this is your unique path, and every step you take is a triumph in itself.

As you stand on the precipice of this 30-day transformation, envision the person you aspire to become. Allow that vision to guide you through the upcoming chapters, knowing that each day is an opportunity for growth, self-discovery, and the creation of a life that resonates with your truest self. Embrace the journey, and may the next 30 days be the beginning of a profound and positive shift in your life.

Part 1

Understanding behavioural Patterns

In the labyrinth of our daily lives, we often navigate through a series of behaviours that shape our experiences, relationships, and ultimately, our destiny. Chapter 1 of "Change Your Life in 30 Days: A Guide to Personal Transformation" sets the stage for a profound exploration into the intricate web of our behavioural patterns. As we embark on this journey of self-discovery, the pivotal first step beckons us to become acutely aware of the subtle nuances that govern our actions, reactions, and choices.

Chapter 1

Becoming Aware of Our behavioural Patterns: A Prelude to Transformation

In the quiet corners of our minds, our behaviours dance to the rhythm of habits cultivated over years—some serving as allies on our journey, while others, perhaps unbeknownst to us, acting as silent saboteurs. This chapter unfolds as a beacon, illuminating the importance of peering into the depths of our behavioural reservoirs, where the key to unlocking personal transformation lies.

The journey commences with a contemplation of the very essence of behaviour—its impact on our lives, relationships, and overarching sense of self. Behaviour, a mosaic of actions and reactions, is the brush with which we paint the canvas of our existence. Delving into this concept sets the tone for an introspective expedition, urging us to question the driving forces behind our choices.

Guiding us through this labyrinth of self-discovery is the beacon of self-reflection and introspection. In a world characterised by constant motion, these tools serve as our compass, inviting us to pause, observe, and unravel the layers of our behavioural tapestry. Through practical exercises carefully curated for self-awareness, we embark on a journey of introspection, shedding light on the subtle intricacies that often escape casual observation.

The power of self-awareness, unveiled in this chapter, lies not only in recognizing our habits but also in understanding the psychological triggers that set them into motion. Triggers, the silent architects of our behaviour, exert a profound influence on our responses to the world around us. Chapter 1 challenges us to uncover these triggers, to dissect their origins, and to equip ourselves with the tools to manage and overcome their influence.

Yet, beneath the surface of triggers lies a deeper exploration—the profound impact of childhood experiences on our present behaviour and perceptions. Chapter 1 urges us to embark on a poignant journey into our past, where the echoes of childhood shape our worldview and mold our adult selves. It's an exploration that requires courage, as we confront the shadows of our past to heal, reframe, and ultimately pave the way for positive change.

As we navigate the landscape of identity and decision-making in the concluding sections of this opening chapter, we unravel the intricate dance between who we believe we are and the choices we make. This exploration prompts a profound question: How does our identity influence the decisions that chart the course of our lives? Chapter 1 serves as a guide, inviting us to scrutinize limiting beliefs and cultivate a positive, empowering self-identity.

In the ever-shifting mosaic of our behavioural patterns, your first chapter is the brushstroke that initiates a masterpiece of personal transformation. With self-awareness as our compass and introspection as our guide, we stand at the threshold, ready to embark on a journey that promises to unravel the mysteries of our behaviours, laying the foundation for change that will resonate through the next 30 days and beyond. The canvas awaits, and the journey of becoming aware of our behavioural patterns unfolds, inviting us to step into the realm of profound self-discovery and transformation.

Exploring the Concept of behaviour and Its Impact on Our Lives: A Profound Journey into Self-Understanding

Within the intricacies of human experience, behaviour emerges as the thread weaving together the narrative of our lives. It's the language through which we express ourselves, the mirror reflecting our innermost thoughts, and the compass guiding our interactions with the world. As we embark on the exploration of behaviour and its profound impact on our lives, we delve into the essence of what shapes our actions, reactions, and the very fabric of our existence.

The Multifaceted Landscape of behaviour

Behaviour, in its simplest form, encompasses the actions and reactions that constitute our daily interactions. However, beneath this apparent simplicity lies a complex and multifaceted landscape. It is a dynamic interplay of conscious and subconscious choices, influenced by an intricate dance between our thoughts, emotions, and external stimuli.

Our behaviours extend beyond mere actions; they encapsulate the responses to the stimuli that life presents. How we react to challenges, celebrate victories, and navigate the ebb and flow of relationships all contribute to the mosaic of our behavioural patterns. To understand behaviour is to embark on a journey through the labyrinth of human nature, a journey that holds the key to unlocking the door to self-discovery and transformation.

The Power of Self-Reflection and Introspection

To explore the concept of behaviour, we must first turn our gaze inward. Self-reflection and introspection emerge as indispensable tools in unraveling the mysteries of our actions. In a world that often prioritizes constant motion, these practices offer the sanctuary of stillness—the opportunity to pause, observe, and inquire into the motivations driving our behaviour.

Self-reflection invites us to question the 'why' behind our actions. Why do certain situations trigger specific responses? Why do I react negatively to a certain stimulus but react ambiguously or even positively to the same stimulant but from a separate source? Why do particular patterns persist in our lives? By contemplating these questions with a spirit of curiosity rather than judgment, we open a gateway to self-awareness.

Introspection, a deeper dive into the inner recesses of our minds, allows us to unearth the subtle nuances that may escape casual observation. It's a journey of honesty and authenticity, a willingness to confront both the light and shadow within. Through these practices, we gain insight into the intricacies of our behavioural patterns, creating a foundation for intentional change.

In the next section, we will look at practical exercises that will increase our self-awareness.

The Unveiling of Psychological Triggers

In the grand tapestry of behaviour, psychological triggers emerge as pivotal threads that shape our responses. Understanding these triggers requires peeling back the layers of our reactions to uncover the roots embedded in our psyche.

Psychological triggers are stimuli that evoke strong emotional responses, often rooted in past experiences. They act as catalysts, setting into motion a chain of reactions that influence our behaviour. Exploring the concept of triggers involves acknowledging their existence, identifying common triggers, and developing strategies to manage and overcome their influence.

Identifying triggers necessitates a heightened level of self-awareness. It involves recognizing patterns of emotional responses and discerning the events or circumstances that precede these reactions. By shining a light on these triggers, we gain the power to respond consciously rather than reactively.

Once identified, the journey continues with the exploration of techniques to manage and overcome triggers. This might involve cultivating mindfulness to interrupt automatic reactions, employing relaxation techniques to soothe heightened emotions, or seeking professional guidance to navigate complex triggers rooted in past trauma.

Understanding and mastering psychological triggers marks a significant milestone in our exploration of behaviour. It empowers us to reclaim agency over our responses, fostering emotional intelligence and resilience in the face of life's challenges.

The Impact of Childhood Experiences on Our Perception

As we venture deeper into the exploration of behaviour, we inevitably encounter the profound influence of childhood experiences on our present selves. Our early years, marked by a myriad of interactions, shape the lens through which we perceive the world. This chapter delves into the complex interplay between past and present, inviting us to examine the footprints left by our formative years.

Childhood experiences serve as the foundation upon which our belief systems, values, and emotional responses are constructed. Positive experiences contribute to a sense of security and self-worth, while negative or traumatic events can imprint lasting imbalances that echo through the years.

Recognizing the impact of these early experiences is not an exercise in blame but an opportunity for healing and growth. It requires a compassionate exploration of our past, acknowledging the wounds that may persist and understanding how they manifest in our adult behaviours.

Healing and reframing past narratives emerge as essential components of this exploration. The process involves revisiting memories with a newfound perspective, extracting lessons from challenges, and embracing the resilience that often arises from overcoming adversity. By reframing our narratives, we pave the way for a more empowered present and future.

In essence, understanding the influence of childhood experiences on behaviour is an act of reclaiming authorship over our stories. It's an acknowledgment of the role these early chapters play in the grand narrative of our lives and an invitation to rewrite subsequent chapters with wisdom and intention. Our behaviours as adults are directly related to our survival strategies as children.

Mary is the younger brother of Sean who is a couple of years older. Sean frequently (in Mary's eyes) picks on her, teases her and generally isn't a nice big brother. Subconsciously Mary tries different approaches to dealing with the situation. She cries and tells her parents who scold Sean, but what happens then? Sean teases her when their parents aren't around so strategy #1 when grown ups are around works fine, but doesn't when they are not there. Enter strategy #2 where she attempts to redirect Sean's behaviour towards her by befriending him and doing nice things for him. If strategy #2 works, it's very likely that Mary will adopt this strategy into her life when confronted with similar situations, making it a habit and eventually a behaviour - becoming the person who always says yes, the one who's a friend to everyone. If it doesn't work, or doesn't work fully, she may employ different strategies until she finds one that works, subconsciously storing it away until a similar situation occurs where she can use it. Thus the impact of the childhood experience impacts our perception of the world and how we interact with it.

The Connection between Identity and Decision Making

Behaviour, intricately woven into the fabric of our identity, emerges as a decisive force in the choices we make. Chapter 4 invites us to explore the symbiotic relationship between identity and decision-making processes, unraveling the threads that bind the essence of who we are to the paths we choose to traverse.

Identity, the amalgamation of our beliefs, values, and self-perception, serves as the compass guiding our decisions. It is the lens through which we interpret the world, influencing the choices that shape our lives. This exploration delves into the intricacies of identity, shedding light on the dynamic interplay between our sense of self and the decisions we make.

Examining the relationship between identity and decision making involves a scrutiny of limiting beliefs—the narratives we internalize that may constrain our choices. These beliefs, often rooted in past experiences or societal conditioning, act as veils that obscure our true potential. Identifying and challenging these limiting beliefs is a critical step toward fostering a more expansive and empowered identity.

Cultivating a positive and empowering self-identity becomes a focal point of this exploration. It is an intentional act of shaping our beliefs and perceptions to align with the person we aspire to be. By recognizing and celebrating our strengths, acknowledging our growth, and embracing a sense of self-worth, we lay the foundation for decisions that resonate with our authentic selves.

In essence, the connection between identity and decision making unveils the profound role our beliefs play in steering the course of our lives

Practical Exercises to Increase Self-Awareness: Navigating the Path to Transformation

In the journey toward personal transformation, self-awareness stands as the cornerstone—a profound understanding of one's thoughts, emotions, and behaviours. As we navigate the labyrinth of our inner selves, practical exercises become indispensable tools, guiding us toward the light of self-discovery. In this exploration, we embark on a journey through a series of practical exercises designed to illuminate the pathways of self-awareness, creating a roadmap for intentional change.

1. Daily Journaling: Unveiling Patterns through Reflection

Journaling, a timeless practice, emerges as a powerful medium for self-awareness. The act of putting pen to paper encourages introspection and contemplation, unveiling patterns that may remain obscured in the hustle of daily life. Start by setting aside a few minutes each day to reflect on your experiences, emotions, and reactions.

Begin with a simple prompt, such as "Today, I felt..." or "In this situation, my response was..." Use the journal to explore the intricacies of your thoughts and feelings. Are there recurring themes? What triggers certain emotions or reactions? As you accumulate entries, patterns may reveal themselves, offering valuable insights into your behavioural tendencies.

The best way to journal ultimately depends on your personal preferences and goals. However, here's a simple and effective structure you can use to start your journal entries:

Date:

Start each entry by noting the date. This helps you track your thoughts and experiences over time.

Heading or a title:

Give your journal entry a brief heading or title that encapsulates the main theme or focus.

Body:

Write freely about your thoughts, feelings, and experiences. You can cover a range of topics, such as:
- Daily Events: Describe what happened during your day.
- Emotions: Explore and express your feelings.
- Reflections: Contemplate on specific events, personal growth, or lessons learned.
- Goals: Discuss your aspirations, progress, or setbacks.
- Gratitude: Note things you are grateful for.

Goals or Intentions:

Set goals or intentions for the next day or reflect on progress toward existing goals.

Positive Takeaways:

Highlight positive aspects or lessons learned, even in challenging situations.

Any Other Sections Relevant to You:

Tailor your journal to your needs. You might include sections like:
- ❖ Quotes: Add inspirational or meaningful quotes.
- ❖ Self-Reflection Questions: Pose questions to yourself for deeper contemplation. (why did I have the response I had to "X"?
- ❖ Achievements: Celebrate accomplishments, big or small.

2. Mindfulness Meditation: Cultivating Present-Moment Awareness

Mindfulness meditation, rooted in ancient traditions, has become a modern-day beacon for cultivating self-awareness. This practice involves directing attention to the present moment, observing thoughts without judgment, and cultivating a heightened awareness of sensations and emotions. Set aside dedicated time each day for mindfulness meditation, allowing yourself to fully immerse in the experience.

Begin with focused breathing, anchoring your attention to the rhythm of inhalation and exhalation. Gradually expand your awareness to encompass the sensations in your body, the sounds in your environment, and the thoughts passing through your mind. The key is non-judgmental observation—acknowledging thoughts and sensations without attachment. Through consistent practice, mindfulness becomes a lens through which you perceive and understand your inner landscape.

There are literally thousands of instructional videos on mindfulness you can learn from on YouTube, Tik Tok, Instagram and other social media platforms that will give you exactly what you need.

3. The Johari Window: Expanding Self-Understanding through Feedback

The Johari Window, a psychological tool developed by Joseph Luft and Harry Ingham, provides a structured framework for self-awareness. It divides self-awareness into four quadrants: the Open Area (known to self and others), the Blind Spot (unknown to self but known to others), the Hidden Area (known to self but unknown to others), and the Unknown Area (unknown to self and others).

To apply the Johari Window, engage in open and honest communication with trusted friends, family members, or colleagues. Seek feedback on your strengths, weaknesses, and how you navigate various situations. This exercise not only expands your self-awareness but also fosters a deeper connection with those who contribute to your Johari Window.

4. Body Scan Exercise: Listening to the Wisdom of Your Body

The body often serves as a reservoir of unspoken wisdom, storing tension, discomfort, and subtle cues that elude conscious awareness. The body scan exercise is a mindfulness practice that involves systematically directing attention to different parts of the body, observing sensations without judgment.

Find a quiet space, either sitting or lying down. Close your eyes and bring attention to your breath, gradually shifting focus to different areas of your body. Notice any tension, warmth, or discomfort. The body scan offers a holistic understanding of how your emotions manifest physically, providing insights into the connection between your mental and physical states.

5. Strengths and Weaknesses Analysis: Embracing Authenticity

Understanding your strengths and weaknesses is fundamental to self-awareness. Create a list of your perceived strengths and weaknesses, considering both professional and personal aspects. Be honest and specific in your assessment. Reflect on instances where these qualities manifested and their impact on your life.

This exercise serves not only as a self-awareness tool but also as a foundation for personal growth. Embrace your strengths, leveraging them in pursuit of your goals. Acknowledge your weaknesses, viewing them not as flaws but as opportunities for development. This practice fosters authenticity, aligning your actions with your true self.

6. Emotional Intelligence Assessment: Navigating the Emotional Landscape

Emotional intelligence, the ability to understand and manage one's own emotions and those of others, is a key component of self-awareness. Various assessments and tools are available to measure emotional intelligence. Engage in one of these assessments, such as the Emotional Intelligence Appraisal by Travis Bradberry and Jean Greaves.

The assessment typically covers areas such as self-awareness, self-regulation, motivation, empathy, and social skills. Use the results as a guide for self-reflection. Identify areas where you excel and those that present opportunities for growth. This exercise not only enhances your understanding of emotional intelligence but also empowers you to navigate the complex terrain of emotions with greater finesse.

7. Values Clarification: Aligning Actions with Core Beliefs

Self-awareness extends beyond understanding thoughts and emotions—it encompasses aligning actions with core values. Take time to clarify your values, considering principles that guide your decisions and define your sense of purpose. Create a list of your top values, ranking them in order of importance.

This exercise serves as a compass, ensuring that your actions align with your deeply held beliefs. Regularly revisit and refine your values, recognizing that they may evolve over time. By consciously aligning your choices with your values, you cultivate a sense of authenticity and purpose in your journey of self-discovery.

8. The 5 Whys: Uncovering Root Causes

Originally a problem-solving technique, the 5 Whys can also be adapted to explore the root causes of behaviours and patterns. When faced with a specific behaviour or response, ask yourself "Why?" Repeat this process five times, delving deeper with each iteration. The goal is to uncover the underlying motivations or beliefs that drive your actions.

For example, if a behaviour involves procrastination, the sequence might unfold as follows:

- Why do I procrastinate? Because I find the task overwhelming.
- Why do I find the task overwhelming? Because I lack clarity on where to start.
- Why do I lack clarity? Because I haven't broken down the task into smaller steps.
- Why haven't I broken down the task? Because I fear making mistakes.
- Why do I fear making mistakes? Because I associate mistakes with failure.

The 5 Whys reveal layers of understanding, guiding you to the root causes that may be influencing your behaviour. This exercise fosters a deeper comprehension of your thought processes and motivations. You may need to go further than the 5 Whys, six, seven, eight or nine. It depends on the behaviour you wish to understand and how long to get to the root cause. Once you hit on the root cause, there is one final question you need to ask yourself: *"what has to happen now for me to get past this particular root cause"*. This is your call to action from inaction.

9. Future Self Visualization: Envisioning Your Ideal Future

Visualization is a potent tool for self-awareness, allowing you to tap into your aspirations and deepest desires. Set aside dedicated time for future self visualization. Close your eyes and envision your ideal self in a specific time frame—whether it's one year, five years, or a decade from now.

Explore the details of your future self—your lifestyle, relationships, career, and overall well-being. Notice the emotions that accompany this visualization. What values and priorities are evident in this future version of yourself? Use this exercise to align your present actions with the trajectory of your aspirations, creating a bridge between your current state and your envisioned future.

10. Personal SWOT Analysis: Assessing Internal Landscapes

A Personal SWOT Analysis is a structured tool used in business to assess Strengths, Weaknesses, Opportunities, and Threats. Applied to personal development, it becomes a valuable instrument for self.

Chapter 2

Uncovering Psychological Triggers - Navigating the Depths of Influence

As we continue our journey of self-discovery in "Change Your Life in 30 Days: A Guide to Personal Transformation," we delve into the intricate realm of Chapter 2, where the focus shifts to the profound exploration of psychological triggers. In the tapestry of our experiences, these triggers are the silent architects shaping our responses, influencing our choices, and, ultimately, guiding the course of our lives. This chapter invites you to embark on a quest to uncover these elusive triggers, understand their psychological underpinnings, and equip yourself with the tools to manage and transcend their influence.

The Dynamics of Psychological Triggers

Psychological triggers are catalysts that evoke strong emotional responses within us. These stimuli often originate from past experiences, shaping our perceptions, beliefs, and behaviours. Much like hidden currents beneath the surface of calm waters, triggers influence the direction of our emotional responses, often steering us toward familiar patterns of reaction.

Understanding psychological triggers is akin to lifting the veil on the subconscious, bringing to light the forces that drive our emotional responses. These triggers can range from specific words, situations, or even the tone of voice to more complex stimuli rooted in past traumas or significant life events. Chapter 2 beckons you to navigate this complex landscape, unraveling the threads that tie your present reactions to the experiences that have left an indelible mark on your psyche.

Identifying Common Triggers and Their Effects

Central to the exploration of psychological triggers is the identification of common stimuli that elicit emotional responses. These triggers may manifest in various aspects of life, from relationships and work environments to personal challenges and aspirations. By recognizing these patterns, you gain a profound insight into the undercurrents shaping your emotional landscape.

Common triggers often surface in situations that mirror past experiences, creating a resonance between the present moment and the emotional imprints of the past. As you uncover these triggers, pay attention to the emotional responses they provoke. Are they rooted in fear, insecurity, or perhaps a desire for control? The effects of triggers are as diverse as the triggers themselves, and understanding these dynamics empowers you to navigate emotional terrain with heightened awareness.

Techniques for Managing and Overcoming Triggers

Armed with the knowledge of your triggers, the next step is to explore techniques for managing and overcoming their influence. Chapter 2 introduces a toolkit of strategies designed to disrupt automatic responses and cultivate a conscious approach to triggers.

Mindfulness, a practice introduced in the previous chapter, emerges as a potent ally in this endeavor. By bringing focused attention to the present moment, mindfulness enables you to observe your thoughts and emotions without immediate judgment. This heightened awareness provides a space for intentional responses rather than reflexive reactions, offering a valuable buffer against the influence of triggers.

Cognitive-behavioural techniques, rooted in the understanding that thoughts influence emotions and behaviours, offers a structured approach to managing triggers. By challenging and reframing negative thought patterns associated with triggers, you reshape the emotional landscape. This process involves questioning the validity of automatic thoughts and consciously choosing alternative, more constructive perspectives.

Identify Automatic Negative Thoughts:

- **Situation**: You find yourself in a challenging or triggering situation, such as receiving critical feedback at work.
- **Automatic Thought**: Identify the automatic negative thought that arises, such as "I'm a failure; I can never do anything right."
- **Challenge the Thought**: Question the validity of this thought. Ask yourself if it's based on evidence or if it's an exaggerated or distorted perception. Consider alternative interpretations, such as acknowledging your areas for improvement without labeling yourself as a failure.
- **Reframe**: Replace the negative thought with a more balanced and constructive one, such as "I received feedback on specific areas where I can improve, and that's an

opportunity for growth. It doesn't define my overall competence."

Gratitude Journaling for Perspective Shift:

- ❖ **Situation**: You experience a triggering event, like a conflict with a friend.
- ❖ **Automatic Thought**: Automatic negative thoughts may include feelings of anger, resentment, or a sense of injustice.
- ❖ **Challenge the Thought**: Start a gratitude journaling exercise. List three things you're grateful for, even in the midst of the triggering situation. This shifts your focus from negativity to positive aspects of your life.
- ❖ **Reframe**: Reframe your perspective by acknowledging that while the triggering event is challenging, there are other positive aspects in your life. This can create a more balanced emotional response and reduce the intensity of negative emotions associated with the trigger.

Behavioral Experimentation for Social Anxiety:

- ❖ **Situation**: You feel anxious about attending a social event due to fear of judgment or rejection.
- ❖ **Automatic Thought**: Automatic thoughts may include "People will think I'm awkward, and no one will want to talk to me."
- ❖ **Challenge the Thought**: Challenge this thought by engaging in a behavioral experiment. Attend the social event with the intention of starting a conversation with at least one person. Pay attention to actual reactions and outcomes.
- ❖ **Reframe**: After the event, evaluate the experience. If you had positive interactions, use that evidence to challenge the automatic thought. Reframe the thought as "I was able to

connect with others, and not everyone perceived me negatively."

These examples illustrate how cognitive-behavioral techniques involve identifying automatic thoughts, challenging their validity, and consciously choosing more constructive perspectives to manage triggers effectively.

Therapeutic interventions, such as exposure therapy or Eye Movement Desensitization and Reprocessing (EMDR), can be valuable tools for individuals grappling with triggers stemming from trauma or deeply ingrained patterns. Seeking professional guidance provides a supportive environment for exploring the origins of triggers and developing personalized strategies for managing their impact.

Navigating the Waters of Emotional Intelligence

At its core, the exploration of psychological triggers aligns with the broader journey of enhancing emotional intelligence. Emotional intelligence involves understanding, managing, and utilizing emotions effectively—a skill set that significantly contributes to personal and interpersonal success.

Chapter 2 serves as a bridge connecting the understanding of triggers to the broader landscape of emotional intelligence. By honing your ability to identify, manage, and overcome triggers, you cultivate emotional resilience, fostering a profound awareness of your own emotional landscape and that of others.

A Personal Voyage of Discovery

As you engage with the content of Chapter 2, consider it not merely as a chapter in a book but as a personal voyage of discovery. The insights gained from uncovering psychological triggers lays the foundation for intentional and transformative change. This chapter invites you to become an active participant in this journey, delving into the depths of your emotional terrain with courage and curiosity.

In the chapters that follow, the tools and insights gained from exploring psychological triggers will continue to weave into the fabric of your transformative experience. As you navigate the waters of self-discovery, remember that each revelation is a step toward empowerment, and each conquered trigger is a triumph in your quest for a more conscious and intentional existence. Welcome to Chapter 2, where the exploration of psychological triggers unfolds—a journey that promises self-awareness, resilience, and the key to unlocking your personal transformation.

Understanding the Psychology Behind Triggers and Their Influence: Decoding the Patterns of Emotional Response

Within the complex web of interconnected threads of human experience, emotions play a central role, acting as the vibrant strands that weave together the narrative of our lives. Within this emotional landscape, triggers emerge as the catalysts that set off intricate patterns of response, influencing our thoughts, actions, and overall well-being. As we embark on the journey of understanding the psychology behind triggers and their profound influence, we delve into the nuances of emotional responses, exploring the roots of triggers and decoding the intricate dance between past experiences and present reactions.

The Nature of Triggers: A Gateway to the Subconscious

Triggers, in psychological terms, are stimuli that evoke strong emotional reactions within an individual. These stimuli can be diverse, ranging from specific words, tones of voice, or environmental cues to more complex and deeply rooted associations tied to past experiences. At their essence, triggers act as gateways to the subconscious, unlocking emotions that may have been dormant or buried beneath the surface.

Understanding triggers involves recognizing that their impact extends beyond the immediate emotional response. Triggers are often linked to implicit memories, stored in the subconscious mind, and connected to past experiences. These experiences may be joyful, traumatic, or anywhere in between, but their influence lingers, shaping the lens through which we interpret and navigate the present.

The Link to Past Experiences: An Emotional Resonance

One of the key aspects of triggers lies in their connection to past experiences. Imagine a scenario where a particular smell transports you instantly to a cherished childhood memory or, conversely, evokes feelings of discomfort associated with a challenging time. Triggers operate in a similar fashion, creating an emotional resonance that links the present moment to the imprints of the past.

This emotional resonance is deeply embedded in our neural pathways, forming associations between stimuli and emotional responses. The brain, in its remarkable capacity to adapt, creates these connections as a way of navigating the complexities of our environment. However, when certain stimuli become associated with heightened emotional states—whether positive or negative—they transform into triggers that influence our emotional landscape.

The Role of the Amygdala: The Emotional Sentinel

To comprehend the psychology behind triggers, we must acquaint ourselves with the amygdala, a small almond-shaped structure deep within the brain. The amygdala serves as a primal emotional sentinel, playing a crucial role in processing and interpreting emotions, particularly those associated with fear and pleasure.

When a potential threat or reward is detected, the amygdala responds rapidly, triggering the release of neurotransmitters and hormones that prepare the body for action. This rapid response, while evolutionarily advantageous for survival, also contributes to the formation of emotional associations and the identification of triggers. The amygdala becomes a repository for emotional memories, influencing our reactions to similar stimuli in the future.

The Formation of Emotional Memory: From Experience to Trigger

The formation of emotional memory involves a complex interplay of brain regions, neurotransmitters, and synaptic connections. When we experience an emotionally charged event, the brain encodes the details of the experience, including sensory information, emotions, and contextual cues. This encoded information is stored in the amygdala and other regions associated with memory.

Over time, as the brain consolidates these memories, certain stimuli become intricately linked to the emotional tone of the experience. For example, a particular song may become associated with a significant life event, creating a trigger that elicits the emotions tied to that event whenever the song is heard. This process of emotional memory formation is a fundamental aspect of understanding the psychology behind triggers.

Categorizing Triggers: From Personal to Universal

Triggers can be categorized into two broad types: personal triggers and universal triggers. Personal triggers are idiosyncratic to an individual, arising from their unique life experiences, traumas, and associations. These triggers are deeply personalized and may not evoke the same responses in others.

On the other hand, universal triggers are stimuli that tend to evoke similar emotional responses across a broad spectrum of individuals. Examples include images of threatening animals, certain facial expressions conveying fear or joy, or loud and sudden noises. These triggers often have evolutionary roots, reflecting shared human experiences and survival instincts.

Understanding the distinction between personal and universal triggers is crucial in deciphering the complexity of emotional responses. While personal triggers may require individualized exploration and healing, universal triggers provide insights into the common threads of human experience.

The Influence of Culture and Conditioning: Shaping Trigger Responses

Culture and societal conditioning play a pivotal role in shaping the landscape of triggers. Cultural norms, values, and expectations contribute to the formation of triggers by influencing the interpretation of events and the emotional significance assigned to certain stimuli.

For example, in cultures where the expression of certain emotions is encouraged or discouraged, individuals may develop triggers associated with the acceptance or suppression of those emotions. Similarly, societal narratives and stereotypes can contribute to the formation of triggers related to identity, self-worth, and belonging.

The influence of culture and conditioning highlights the dynamic nature of triggers—they are not static entities but evolving aspects of our psychological landscape. Recognizing the impact of cultural factors is essential for a comprehensive understanding of triggers and their influence on emotional responses.

The Emotional Spectrum of Triggers: From Positive to Negative

Triggers encompass a broad spectrum of emotional responses, spanning from positive triggers that evoke joy, love, or nostalgia to negative triggers associated with fear, anger, or sadness. Positive triggers often serve as sources of inspiration, motivation, and comfort, contributing to the richness of human experience.

Negative triggers, however, can pose challenges by eliciting stress, anxiety, or other adverse emotions. These triggers may be linked to past traumas, unresolved issues, or unmet needs. Exploring negative triggers involves a delicate process of introspection and, in some cases, therapeutic support to navigate the emotional terrain and foster healing.

Understanding the emotional spectrum of triggers is crucial for harnessing their positive potential and mitigating the impact of negative triggers. By cultivating awareness of the full range of trigger responses, individuals can develop strategies for emotional regulation and resilience.

Managing Triggers: A Path to Emotional Regulation

The journey of understanding triggers extends beyond mere awareness to the active management of their influence. Emotional regulation becomes a key component of navigating triggers, empowering individuals to respond consciously rather than reactively. In this chapter, we'll explore various techniques and strategies for managing triggers, offering practical insights into building emotional resilience and fostering a more intentional approach to life.

Unraveling the Threads of Emotional Influence

Understanding the psychology behind triggers is a profound exploration into the intricate threads of emotional influence that shape our lives. Triggers, rooted in the interplay of past experiences, emotional memory, and the complexities of the human brain, hold the key to unlocking patterns of response and reaction.

As we unravel the threads of emotional influence, we gain insights not only into our own triggers but also into the shared aspects of human experience. The journey of understanding triggers is a continuous process, inviting us to navigate the depths of our emotional landscape with curiosity, compassion, and a commitment to self-discovery.

In Chapter 2, we embark on a guided exploration of practical techniques for uncovering, understanding, and managing triggers. The insights gained from this journey will serve as valuable tools for the transformative endeavors that lie ahead in our 30-day guide to personal transformation. Welcome to the intricate world of triggers—a landscape where self-awareness becomes the compass, and intentional responses pave the way to emotional resilience and lasting change.

Identifying Common Triggers and Their Effects on behaviour: Decoding the Blueprint of Emotional Responses

In the intricate dance of human emotions, triggers emerge as the choreographers, directing the patterns of our responses with precision. These triggers, often subtle and nuanced, are the stimuli that elicit powerful emotional reactions, shaping our behaviour in profound ways. As we embark on the journey of identifying common triggers and unraveling their effects on behaviour, we delve into the blueprint of emotional responses, exploring the interconnected web that binds stimuli, emotions, and actions.

The Spectrum of Common Triggers: A Kaleidoscope of Influences

Common triggers span a vast spectrum, ranging from external stimuli in our immediate environment to internal thoughts and memories. Identifying these triggers involves developing a keen awareness of the factors that evoke emotional responses. Some triggers are universal, resonating across diverse individuals, while others are deeply personal, rooted in individual experiences and histories.

Environmental Triggers: These are stimuli present in our surroundings that can evoke emotional responses. Examples include loud noises, crowded spaces, specific scents, or particular types of lighting. Environmental triggers often tap into our sensory experiences, creating emotional responses linked to the immediate context.

Social Triggers: Interactions with others can serve as potent triggers, influencing our emotional states and subsequent behaviours. Social triggers may arise from specific communication styles, body language, or even the dynamics of group interactions. For instance, criticism, rejection, or praise can act as powerful social triggers, shaping our behaviour in social settings.

Cognitive Triggers: Internal thoughts and beliefs can also act as triggers, influencing our emotional responses and behaviours. These cognitive triggers may stem from self-talk, automatic thoughts, or ingrained beliefs about ourselves and the world. Identifying and understanding these thought patterns is crucial for unraveling their impact on behaviour.

Memory-Related Triggers: Past experiences, memories, and associations can act as triggers, resurfacing emotions tied to specific events. A familiar place, a particular date, or even a specific word may trigger memories that influence our present emotional state and behaviour. Unraveling the threads of memory-related triggers involves exploring the emotional imprints left by past experiences.

Routine and Habit Triggers: Repetitive behaviours and routines can become associated with specific emotional states, acting as triggers that influence our behaviour. For example, the routine of grabbing a cup of coffee in the morning may be linked to feelings of comfort or anticipation, shaping our behaviour as we go about our daily rituals.

The Interplay of Triggers and Emotional Responses: A Symphony of Influence

Identifying common triggers is only the first step; understanding their effects on behaviour requires an exploration of the intricate symphony of emotions and actions that follows. Triggers serve as catalysts, setting off a cascade of emotional responses that, in turn, shape our behaviour. The interplay between triggers and emotional responses is dynamic and multifaceted, with each trigger contributing to the composition of our behavioural symphony.

Emotional Responses to Triggers: Triggers evoke a spectrum of emotions, ranging from joy and excitement to fear and anger. For example, a social trigger such as public speaking may evoke anxiety, while a routine trigger like the smell of a favorite meal may elicit feelings of warmth and anticipation. Recognizing the emotional responses tied to specific triggers provides valuable insights into the influence they wield over our behaviour.

Behavioural Patterns Unveiled: The effects of triggers manifest in our behaviours, shaping the way we respond to the emotional cues they evoke. Social triggers may lead to behaviours such as withdrawal, seeking reassurance, or adopting defensive postures. Environmental triggers can prompt behaviours like avoidance or seeking comfort. By closely observing our behavioural patterns, we gain a clearer understanding of the influence exerted by common triggers.

Automatic vs. Conscious Responses: The interplay between triggers and behaviour often involves a distinction between automatic and conscious responses. Automatic responses are instinctive reactions that arise without conscious deliberation, driven by the emotional intensity of the trigger. On the other hand, conscious responses involve intentional choices and actions based on a more thoughtful and reasoned approach. Identifying whether our behaviours are automatic or conscious provides a nuanced understanding of the impact of triggers on decision-making.

Patterns of Coping and Adaptation: Triggers also shape our coping mechanisms and adaptive strategies. Some individuals may engage in avoidance behaviours to cope with certain triggers, while others may seek support or employ relaxation techniques. The identification of these coping patterns sheds light on our unique ways of navigating the emotional terrain influenced by triggers.

Examples of Common Triggers and Their behavioural Effects

To illustrate the complex interplay between common triggers and behavioural effects, let's explore a few examples across different categories:

Environmental Trigger: Loud Noises

- Emotional Response: Anxiety or startle response.
- Behavioural Effect: Seeking refuge in a quiet space, covering ears, or displaying signs of nervousness.

Social Trigger: Criticism from a Colleague

- Emotional Response: Hurt, defensiveness, or frustration.
- Behavioural Effect: Defensive reactions, withdrawal from social interactions, or seeking reassurance.

Cognitive Trigger: Negative Self-Talk

- Emotional Response: Low self-esteem, sadness, or frustration.
- Behavioural Effect: Avoidance of challenges, reluctance to take risks, or self-isolation.

Memory-Related Trigger: Anniversary of a Traumatic Event

- Emotional Response: Sorrow, anxiety, or fear.
- Behavioural Effect: Avoidance of reminders, heightened vigilance, or seeking support.

Routine and Habit Trigger: Morning Coffee Ritual

- Emotional Response: Comfort, anticipation, or pleasure.
- behavioural Effect: Engaging in the ritual, associating the activity with a positive start to the day.

Unveiling the Threads of Influence

Identifying common triggers and understanding their effects on behaviour unveils the intricate threads of influence that shape our emotional responses and actions. Triggers, whether environmental, social, cognitive, memory-related, or routine-based, act as architects of behaviour, crafting the intricate patterns of our responses to the world.

As we navigate the landscape of triggers, armed with self-awareness and proactive strategies, we gain agency over our behavioural symphony. The journey of unraveling the effects of common triggers becomes a transformative exploration, leading to enhanced emotional resilience, adaptive coping mechanisms, and intentional responses to the ever-changing tapestry of human experience. Welcome to the exploration of triggers—a realm where self-discovery becomes a compass, and understanding paves the way to mindful and purposeful living.

Techniques for Managing and Overcoming Triggers: A Journey to Emotional Mastery

In the intricate tapestry of human emotions, triggers act as invisible threads, weaving patterns of response that shape our behaviour. Understanding triggers is only the first step; the true empowerment lies in the ability to manage and overcome their influence. As we embark on the exploration of techniques for mastering triggers, we delve into a transformative journey that involves mindfulness, cognitive restructuring, resilience-building, and a nuanced understanding of the self.

1. Mindful Awareness: Navigating Triggers with Presence

At the heart of managing triggers lies the practice of mindful awareness—a timeless technique rooted in ancient contemplative traditions. Mindfulness involves cultivating a heightened state of present-moment awareness, allowing individuals to observe thoughts, emotions, and triggers without immediate reactivity.

Begin by anchoring your attention to the breath. In moments of trigger activation, consciously bring your focus to the sensations of breathing, grounding yourself in the present. This intentional shift in attention creates a space between the trigger and your automatic response, offering an opportunity for conscious choice.

As you observe the trigger without judgment, explore the physical sensations and emotions associated with it. Rather than succumbing to reactive patterns, mindfulness enables you to respond with clarity and intention. With consistent practice, mindfulness becomes a powerful tool for navigating the intricate terrain of triggers, fostering resilience and emotional mastery.

2. Cognitive Restructuring: Rewiring Thought Patterns

Cognitive restructuring is a cognitive-behavioural technique that empowers individuals to challenge and reframe automatic negative thoughts associated with triggers. By reshaping the interpretations of triggering events, individuals can modify their emotional responses and subsequent behaviours.

When a trigger activates, pause and identify the thoughts accompanying the emotional response. These thoughts are often automatic and may contribute to heightened emotional intensity. Challenge the validity of these thoughts by asking questions such as:

- ❖ Is this thought based on facts or assumptions?
- ❖ What evidence supports or contradicts this thought?
- ❖ How might someone else view this situation?

Once you've identified and challenged the negative thoughts, consciously reframe them into more balanced and realistic perspectives. For example, if the trigger involves a fear of failure, reframe the thought from "I will definitely fail" to "I may face challenges, but I can learn and grow from the experience."

Cognitive restructuring is a process of rewiring thought patterns, empowering you to approach triggers with a more adaptive and constructive mindset.

3. Resilience Building: Strengthening the Emotional Core

Building resilience is a holistic approach to managing triggers, focusing on enhancing one's ability to bounce back from challenging experiences. Resilience involves cultivating emotional strength, adaptability, and coping mechanisms that foster a sense of mastery over triggers.

Engage in activities that nurture emotional well-being, such as regular exercise, adequate sleep, and a balanced diet. Physical health forms a foundation for emotional resilience, providing the energy and stamina needed to navigate triggers effectively.

Develop a support network of trusted friends, family members, or colleagues. Social connections serve as buffers against the impact of triggers, providing perspectives, empathy, and shared experiences. Communicate openly about triggers and enlist support when needed, fostering a sense of community in your resilience-building journey.

Practice self-compassion by cultivating a kind and understanding relationship with yourself. Acknowledge that everyone faces challenges and triggers, and it's okay to seek help or take a break when needed. Self-compassion creates a supportive internal environment, reducing the intensity of trigger-induced emotions.

Set realistic goals and expectations, recognizing that setbacks and challenges are part of the human experience. Approach goals with a growth mindset, viewing obstacles as opportunities for learning and development. Resilience flourishes when individuals embrace challenges with a sense of adaptability and perseverance.

4. Progressive Exposure: Gradual Confrontation of Triggers

Progressive exposure is a therapeutic technique that involves gradually exposing oneself to triggers in a controlled and systematic manner. This approach is particularly beneficial for individuals facing phobias, anxieties, or intense emotional responses linked to specific triggers.

Create a hierarchy of trigger-related situations, ranging from less distressing to more distressing. Begin by exposing yourself to the least distressing situation, allowing time to habituate to the associated emotions. As comfort and familiarity increase, gradually progress to more challenging scenarios on the hierarchy. Where prudent, complete this strategy with a trained professional.

Throughout the exposure process, practice relaxation techniques such as deep breathing or visualization to manage heightened emotional states. The goal is not immediate elimination of discomfort but rather a gradual desensitization to the trigger, empowering individuals to face challenging situations with increasing resilience.

Progressive exposure fosters a sense of control over triggers and transforms avoidance behaviours into intentional confrontation, leading to emotional mastery and reduced reactivity.

5. Acceptance and Commitment Therapy (ACT): Embracing the Present Moment

Acceptance and Commitment Therapy (ACT) is a therapeutic approach that encourages individuals to accept their thoughts and feelings while committing to actions aligned with their values. This mindfulness-based technique is particularly effective in managing triggers by promoting psychological flexibility and resilience.

When confronted with a trigger, practice mindfulness by observing and accepting the associated thoughts and emotions without judgment. Recognize that discomfort is a natural part of the human experience, and resisting it may intensify the emotional impact.

Clarify your values—what matters most to you in life. Commit to actions that align with these values, even in the presence of triggers. This commitment empowers individuals to move forward purposefully, transcending the immediate influence of triggers and cultivating a meaningful life.

Practice cognitive defusion, a technique in ACT that involves creating distance from distressing thoughts. Rather than becoming entangled in the content of triggering thoughts, view them as passing events in the mind. This shift in perspective reduces the emotional grip of triggers, allowing for greater emotional flexibility.

6. *Mind-Body Techniques: Connecting the Physical and Emotional*

Mind-body techniques bridge the gap between physical and emotional experiences, providing tools for managing triggers through conscious engagement with the body. These techniques encompass practices such as deep breathing, progressive muscle relaxation, and biofeedback.

Deep breathing exercises involve intentional inhalation and exhalation, calming the nervous system and reducing the physiological response to triggers. Practice diaphragmatic breathing by inhaling deeply through the nose, allowing the abdomen to expand, and exhaling slowly through pursed lips.

Progressive muscle relaxation entails systematically tensing and relaxing muscle groups, promoting awareness of bodily sensations and releasing tension. Begin by tensing and relaxing different muscle groups, progressively moving from head to toe.

Biofeedback involves monitoring physiological responses to triggers, such as heart rate or skin conductance, and learning to regulate these responses consciously. Biofeedback devices provide real-time feedback, enhancing awareness and control over the body's stress responses.

By integrating mind-body techniques into daily practices, you gain a holistic approach to managing triggers, fostering a harmonious connection between mental and physical well-being.

Empowering Transformation Through Mastery

In this evolving dance with triggers, the journey of mastering and overcoming their influence becomes a transformative exploration. Mindful awareness, cognitive restructuring, resilience building, progressive exposure, Acceptance and Commitment Therapy (ACT), and mind-body techniques form a comprehensive toolkit for individuals seeking to navigate the complexities of triggers with intention and resilience.

As you embark on this journey, recognize that mastery over triggers is not about eliminating challenges but rather about cultivating a conscious and empowered relationship with them. Each technique offers a unique perspective and set of skills, contributing to the holistic framework of emotional mastery.

Welcome to the realm of transformation—a space where triggers become stepping stones, and the journey toward emotional empowerment unfolds with every mindful breath, reframed thought, and resilient choice. In your pursuit of mastery, may you discover the strength and wisdom to navigate triggers with grace, leading to a life characterized by intentional living and profound self-discovery!

Chapter 3

The Influence of Childhood on Our Perception - Nurturing Seeds, Shaping Horizons

In the symphony of human existence, childhood acts as the initial movement—a foundational melody that echoes through the corridors of our lives. As we step into Chapter 3, we embark on a profound exploration of "The Influence of Childhood on Our Perception." This chapter unravels the intricate threads connecting early experiences to the lens through which we perceive the world, examining the profound impact of our formative years on beliefs, behaviours, and the very fabric of our reality.

Examining the Role of Childhood Experiences: Seeds of Our Worldview

Childhood experiences form the soil from which the roots of our worldview emerge. This examination invites us to traverse the landscapes of our early years, acknowledging the significance of moments that shaped our understanding of self, others, and the intricate tapestry of life. Like seeds planted in fertile ground, these experiences take root, influencing the narratives that unfold in the garden of our perception.

From the warmth of nurturing relationships to the shadows of adversity, every encounter contributes to the complex interplay of emotions and beliefs that color our worldview. Chapter 3 beckons us to explore the nuances of this interplay, recognizing that the echoes of our childhood experiences resound in the choices we make, the relationships we form, and the way we navigate the vast terrain of human connection.

Recognizing the Impact of Early Experiences: The Imprint on Beliefs and behaviours

The impact of early experiences reverberates beyond the realm of memory; it imprints itself on the very core of our being. This chapter urges us to recognize the enduring influence of these imprints on our beliefs and behaviours. Whether bathed in the sunlight of positive affirmations or weathered by the storms of adversity, our early experiences mold the clay of our identity. You might recall from our earlier chapter the story of Mary and her older brother Sean and how those experiences shaped the strategies she would go on to employ in adult life.

We delve into the steps between formative moments and the beliefs we hold about ourselves and the world. The seeds of encouragement sow the fields of self-confidence, while the weeds of criticism may cast shadows on the landscape of self-worth. By acknowledging the impact of early experiences, we gain insight into the origins of our beliefs, paving the way for intentional cultivation and transformation.

Healing and Reframing Past Narratives: A Journey to Positive Change

Amidst the exploration of childhood's influence, Chapter 3 extends an invitation to embark on a journey of healing and reframing. Here, we confront the narratives woven in the loom of our past, discerning the threads that no longer serve our growth. Healing involves acknowledging wounds, embracing vulnerability, and cultivating the resilience to transcend the limitations imposed by early experiences.

The power to reframe past narratives lies within our grasp. This chapter guides us through the process of consciously rewriting the stories we tell ourselves—stories that may have been scripted in the language of limitation. By reframing, we illuminate the corners of our perception, casting light on new possibilities and empowering positive change.

As we navigate this chapter, may we approach the exploration of childhood's influence with curiosity and compassion. The landscapes of our early experiences are rich and varied, containing both shadows and sunlight. Through understanding, recognition, and the transformative alchemy of healing, we embark on a journey towards a more empowered, intentional, and resilient existence.

Welcome to Chapter 3—an odyssey into the realms of our past, where the seeds of perception were sown and the roots of self took hold. May this exploration unveil the wisdom hidden in the soil of our childhood, guiding us toward a future shaped by conscious choice and the transformative power of reframed narratives.

Examining the Role of Childhood Experiences in Shaping Our Worldview: A Deep Dive into the Crucible of Perception

The tapestry of our lives is woven with threads of experiences, emotions, and memories, and at the heart of this intricate composition lies the crucible of childhood – a realm where the seeds of perception are sown, cultivated, and eventually sprout into the complex fabric of our worldview. This exploration of the role of childhood experiences is not a mere retrospective journey; it is a deep dive into the crucible of perception, where the echoes of the past reverberate through the corridors of our present selves, shaping how we interpret the world around us.

Childhood, often referred to as the formative years, is a melting pot where the foundations of our identity and belief systems are laid. The warmth of nurturing relationships, the challenges of adversity, and the kaleidoscope of diverse experiences all contribute to the complexity of our worldview. Imagine this crucible as a cauldron of alchemy, where the raw materials of innocence and curiosity undergo transformation, emerging as the complex alloy of beliefs that will guide us through the landscapes of adulthood.

To understand the profound impact of childhood experiences, we must envision this journey as a multifaceted exploration that encompasses the psychological, emotional, and sociological dimensions of our existence. It is a journey that demands a nuanced understanding of the dynamics at play, acknowledging that every brushstroke on the canvas of perception is imbued with the hues of familial relationships, cultural influences, and societal norms.

Picture the dynamics of family relationships as the first strokes on the canvas – broad strokes that lay the foundation of our emotional landscape. The warmth of parental love becomes a vibrant hue, infusing our worldview with shades of security, self-worth, and trust. Conversely, the cold winds of adversity may introduce darker tones, casting shadows that shape a more guarded and cautious outlook on the canvas of our understanding.

In this crucible, cultural influences act as the palette from which we draw inspiration in painting the landscape of our perception. The rich tapestry of cultural experiences infuses diversity and vibrancy into the fabric of our beliefs. It is in these cultural brushstrokes that we find the colors of traditions, values, and perspectives that contribute to the mosaic of our worldview. The crucible becomes a melting pot, blending various cultural elements into the alloy of our identity.

Societal norms, akin to the underlying structure of the canvas, provide the framework that shapes the contours of our beliefs. The societal lens through which we view success, failure, relationships, and self-worth becomes an integral part of our perceptual apparatus. As we examine the role of childhood experiences, we must navigate through the societal constructs that influence the way we interpret the world, recognizing the subtle yet powerful impact of collective expectations and norms.

The exploration of this melting pot requires a deep dive into the recesses of memory, emotions, and imprints that linger beneath the surface. It is an archaeological excavation, an unraveling of the layers that have accumulated over the years. Each memory, each emotion, each imprint holds significance in the construction of our personal narratives. By understanding the nuances of these experiences, we gain insight into the roots of our beliefs and the filters through which we interpret the present.

Navigating the terrain of examining childhood's role in shaping our worldview demands a willingness to confront both the shadows and the light that dance in the corridors of memory. The narrative of our early years unfolds in a memory woven with threads of joy and sorrow, love and pain. Each stitch forges the framework through which we navigate the landscapes of adulthood, and each chapter becomes a verse in the lyrical composition of our lives.

As we embark on this exploration, it is crucial to extend a compassionate understanding to ourselves. The seeds planted in childhood are not stagnant; they continue to germinate and bear fruit throughout our lives. This understanding becomes a compass, guiding us through the pathways of memory – some sweet and ripe, others still in the process of maturation.

In this journey, we are both archaeologists and artists, excavating the layers of our past while actively engaging in the ongoing creation of our present and future. The canvas of our perception is not static; it is a living, breathing masterpiece that evolves with each new experience, each shift in perspective.

To truly fathom the impact of childhood experiences on our worldview, we must recognize that this exploration is not confined to the realms of psychology alone. It is a synthesis of the psychological, emotional, and sociological elements that converge to shape the lens through which we interpret reality. The crucible becomes a meeting point of disciplines, where the narratives of self and society intersect and intertwine.

As we navigate the corridors of memory and emotion, let us approach the examination of childhood's role with curiosity and compassion. Like explorers charting uncharted waters, we may encounter islands of resilience and oceans of vulnerability. It is through this exploration that we gain a richer understanding of ourselves and the intricate dance between the past and present. Examining the role of childhood experiences in shaping our worldview is not merely a retrospective exercise but a dynamic journey that encompasses the realms of psychology, sociology, and personal narrative. By navigating this complex terrain, we empower ourselves to consciously choose the beliefs and perspectives that align with our present aspirations and values. This is the voyage of self-discovery, where the currents of the past propel us towards the shores of a consciously crafted future.

Recognizing the Impact of Early Experiences on Our Beliefs and behaviours: Navigating the Tapestry of Self

The journey of self-discovery is a multifaceted odyssey, and at its core lies the recognition that the echoes of early experiences reverberate through the very fabric of our beliefs and behaviours. To recognize the impact of these formative encounters is to embark on an exploration of a detailed pattern that shapes our identity. Early experiences, like brushstrokes on the canvas of our lives, imprint themselves deeply, molding the clay of our beliefs and sculpting the contours of our behaviours.

Early experiences are the architects of our beliefs about self-worth, competence, and deservingness. These foundational beliefs often find their roots in the soil of childhood, where the seeds of identity are sown. Positive affirmations, encouragement, and a supportive environment become the nurturing elements that foster a sense of self-confidence, agency, and resilience. In contrast, experiences of criticism, neglect, or adversity can cast shadows on our beliefs, shaping a narrative of self-doubt or unworthiness.

The impact of early experiences extends beyond the realm of beliefs, influencing the intricate dance of behaviours that characterize our daily lives. These behavioural patterns, intricately woven into the tapestry of our existence, bear the fingerprints of the lessons learned and the emotional tone set during our formative years. How we navigate relationships, respond to challenges, and approach success or failure is deeply influenced by the scripts written in the chapters of our early experiences.

To recognize the impact of early experiences is to navigate the landscape of memory and emotion, exploring the links connecting past events to present behaviours. It involves unraveling the layers of conditioning, understanding the narratives that have shaped our responses, and gaining clarity on the origins of deeply ingrained habits. By shining a light on these connections, we empower ourselves to consciously choose the beliefs and behaviours that align with our present aspirations and values.

The recognition of early experiences as powerful shapers of beliefs and behaviours demands a willingness to confront the complexities of our past. It invites us to be both explorers and storytellers, uncovering the layers of memory while weaving a narrative that brings coherence to our understanding of self. As we delve into this recognition, we may encounter both the shadows and the light that dance within the corridors of memory.

The dynamics of family relationships play a pivotal role in shaping the landscape of early experiences. The family, often the first social unit we encounter, becomes the forge where the initial strokes of our identity are painted. The quality of parental guidance, the nature of sibling relationships, and the overall emotional tone within the family become significant factors in the alchemy of early experiences.

Positive familial dynamics, characterized by love, support, and encouragement, lay the groundwork for a belief in one's capabilities and a sense of security in the world. On the other hand, adverse family dynamics marked by conflict, criticism, or neglect may give rise to beliefs rooted in fear, self-doubt, or a pervasive sense of insecurity.

Cultural influences, much like a subtle undercurrent, further shape the contours of early experiences. The cultural milieu in which we are immersed introduces additional layers to the tapestry of beliefs and behaviours. Cultural norms, societal expectations, and prevalent values become influential elements in the formation of our identity. Early experiences within a specific cultural context contribute to the lens through which we interpret the world and define our roles within it.

Recognizing the impact of early experiences involves acknowledging the societal constructs that influence our beliefs and behaviours. These societal norms, often transmitted through various channels such as media, education, and community, serve as the backdrop against which our personal narratives unfold. The societal lens through which we view success, failure, relationships, and self-worth becomes an integral part of our perceptual apparatus.

As we navigate this recognition, it is essential to approach the exploration with a compassionate understanding of ourselves. Early experiences are not static; they continue to shape and influence us, even as we navigate the complexities of adulthood. By recognizing the impact of these experiences, we create a bridge between our past and present selves, fostering a deeper connection with the roots of our beliefs and behaviours.

The recognition of early experiences as significant influencers opens the door to intentional change and growth. It is an acknowledgment that while the past has left imprints, we hold the agency to rewrite the scripts that no longer serve our growth. Therapeutic modalities, self-reflection, and conscious awareness become tools for excavating and reshaping the narratives that shape our self-perception. Recognizing the impact of early experiences on our beliefs and behaviours is an integral step in the journey of self-discovery. It is a journey that requires courage, curiosity, and self-compassion. By delving into the nuances of our early experiences, we gain a deeper understanding of the roots of our beliefs and behaviours, empowering us to consciously shape the narrative of our lives. This becomes the exploration of self, where the recognition of the past becomes a compass guiding us towards a future characterized by intentional growth and authentic self-expression.

Healing and Reframing Past Narratives to Facilitate Positive Change: The Art of Transformative Self-Discovery

The human journey is an intricate tapestry woven with threads of joy and sorrow, triumphs and tribulations. At the heart of this tapestry lie the narratives we construct about our past – stories that shape our identity, influence our beliefs, and mold our behaviours. Yet, not all stories are empowering or conducive to growth. Some narratives may carry the weight of pain, limiting beliefs, and unhealed wounds. In recognizing the profound impact of these narratives, we embark on a journey of healing and reframing – an artful exploration that holds the key to facilitating positive change in our lives.

Understanding the Narrative Landscape: Unveiling the Power of Stories

Our lives are narratives in motion, composed of stories that we tell ourselves about who we are, where we come from, and what we are capable of becoming. These narratives are often shaped by our experiences, both uplifting and challenging, and they become the lens through which we interpret the world. However, not all narratives serve our well-being. Some stories may be tinged with pain, regret, or self-limiting beliefs, creating a narrative landscape that hinders personal growth.

The recognition of the narrative landscape as a dynamic force in our lives is the first step towards healing and positive change. These narratives are not fixed; they are living, breathing entities that can be reshaped and reimagined. By understanding the power of stories, we gain agency over our own narrative, empowering us to engage in the transformative work of healing and reframing.

Healing: A Journey into Self-Compassion and Wholeness

The journey of healing is an odyssey into the realms of self-compassion, acknowledgment, and acceptance. It involves turning towards the wounds of the past with a compassionate gaze, recognizing that healing begins with acknowledging the pain we carry. This journey is not about erasing the past but about fostering a deep sense of understanding and self-compassion.

To embark on the path of healing is to become both the healer and the healed. It is an act of self-love that acknowledges the resilience inherent in confronting wounds and allowing the scars to tell a story of survival. Healing is a process that requires patience, gentleness, and an unwavering commitment to one's own well-being.

Therapeutic modalities, such as psychotherapy, mindfulness practices, and expressive arts, become tools in the hands of the healing seeker. These modalities provide spaces for exploration, expression, and understanding, offering a bridge between the conscious mind and the layers of emotions stored in the body. Through these practices, individuals gain insights into the roots of their pain, fostering a sense of liberation as they release the emotional burdens they've carried.

Reframing: Crafting a Narrative of Empowerment

While healing addresses the wounds, reframing involves consciously reshaping the narratives that have emerged from those wounds. It is an intentional act of storytelling that moves beyond victimhood and embraces empowerment. Reframing invites individuals to view their past through a different lens, one that emphasizes strength, growth, and the lessons gleaned from adversity.

The art of reframing is akin to being both an author and a protagonist in one's life story. It is an act of reclaiming agency over the narrative, recognizing that the meaning we ascribe to our experiences profoundly influences our present and future. Reframing involves identifying the limiting beliefs embedded in our narratives and consciously replacing them with empowering perspectives.

Cognitive restructuring, a cornerstone of reframing, entails challenging and changing negative thought patterns. This process involves examining automatic thoughts, identifying cognitive distortions, and cultivating a more balanced and constructive mindset. Through cognitive restructuring, individuals can challenge self-limiting beliefs, fostering a mental environment conducive to positive change.

Narrative therapy, another powerful tool in the reframing process, involves externalizing problems and collaboratively crafting alternative narratives. By externalizing challenges, individuals gain distance from the issue, allowing them to view it from a fresh perspective. Together with a therapist or through self-reflection, individuals can co-author narratives that emphasize resilience, resourcefulness, and growth.

The Intersection of Healing and Reframing: A Synergistic Dance

Healing and reframing are not isolated endeavors but rather interconnected facets of a transformative journey. As wounds are tended to, and the narrative landscape undergoes intentional reshaping, a synergistic dance unfolds. Healing creates the fertile ground upon which reframing can flourish, and reframing, in turn, reinforces the healing process by infusing narratives with resilience and empowerment.

The synergy between healing and reframing becomes particularly potent when individuals engage in practices that foster holistic well-being. Mindfulness and self-compassion practices, for example, provide a bridge between the emotional and cognitive realms, allowing individuals to simultaneously nurture their emotional wounds and reshape their cognitive perspectives. This holistic approach acknowledges the interconnectedness of mind, body, and spirit in the transformative journey.

As individuals traverse the terrain of healing and reframing, they often unearth untapped reservoirs of strength and resilience within themselves. The process is not linear; it involves moments of triumph and setbacks, moments of clarity and confusion. Yet, with each step, individuals move closer to a narrative that reflects their authentic selves – a narrative characterized by self-compassion, empowerment, and a profound understanding of their own capacity for growth.

Facilitating Positive Change: The Emergence of Empowered Living

Healing and reframing pave the way for positive change by fostering a shift in how individuals perceive themselves and their life stories. The emergence of empowered living is marked by intentional choices, authentic self-expression, and a deep sense of agency over one's narrative. As individuals integrate the lessons learned from their healing journey and infuse their reframed narratives with empowerment, they become active participants in the co-creation of their lives.

Positive change is not confined to specific behaviours or external circumstances; it emanates from a fundamental shift in the core beliefs that shape one's identity. The reframed narrative becomes a compass guiding individuals towards choices aligned with their values, aspirations, and a vision of a flourishing future. The healing journey, woven into the fabric of reframed narratives, becomes a source of inspiration rather than a hindrance.

The transformative power of healing and reframing extends beyond the individual to ripple into relationships, communities, and the broader tapestry of humanity. Empowered individuals, grounded in their healed and reframed narratives, contribute to the collective narrative of resilience and possibility. Their stories become beacons of hope, inviting others to embark on their own journeys of self-discovery and positive change.

The Artful Tapestry of Transformation

Healing and reframing past narratives to facilitate positive change is a nuanced and artful process. It involves the delicate interplay of self-compassion, intentional narrative crafting, and a commitment to growth. The journey is not about denying or dismissing the past but about embracing it with an open heart and a courageous spirit.

As people engage in the transformative work of healing and reframing, they become artists of their own tapestries. The threads of pain and resilience, woven together with intention and mindfulness, create a masterpiece that tells a story of transformation and empowerment. The artful tapestry of transformation is a testament to the human capacity for resilience, growth, and the alchemical process of turning wounds into wisdom.

Chapter 4

The Connection between Identity and Decision Making

In the complexity of our lives, decisions are the threads that weave the narrative of our journey. At the core of each choice lies a dynamic relationship between our sense of self and the intricate processes that guide our decisions. This chapter embarks on an exploration into the profound connection between identity and decision-making, unraveling the subtle nuances that influence the paths we choose. Together, we will delve into the depths of this relationship, peeling back the layers to uncover the impact of limiting beliefs on our choices. As we navigate this exploration, we will illuminate the transformative potential that lies in cultivating a positive and empowering self-identity. Join me on this insightful journey as we navigate the intricate terrain where the essence of who we are converges with the decision-making processes, and discover how fostering a resilient and positive self-perception can become a compass for intentional and fulfilling choices.

Exploring the Relationship between Identity and Decision-Making Processes: The Tapestry of Self in Choices

The intricate dance of decision-making unfolds against the backdrop of our identity—a mosaic of experiences, beliefs, and perceptions that shape the very core of who we are. In exploring the profound relationship between identity and decision-making processes, we embark on a journey to unravel the threads that bind these two fundamental aspects of human experience.

At the heart of this exploration lies the recognition that our identity, often molded by a myriad of influences, acts as a guiding force in the decisions we make. The process of decision-making is not a detached, rational endeavor but rather a deeply nuanced interplay between conscious and subconscious elements of our identity.

To understand this relationship, we must first appreciate the multidimensional nature of identity. It encompasses not only our self-concept, shaped by personal experiences and self-perception but also the social, cultural, and contextual facets that contribute to the kaleidoscope of who we are. Our identity is both a product and a producer of our decisions, creating a dynamic feedback loop that influences the choices we face and the choices we make.

As we navigate the terrain of identity and decision-making, we encounter the subtle dance between values, beliefs, and motivations. Our values, the principles and ideals that hold significance to us, serve as guiding stars in the decision-making constellation. They act as a compass, directing us toward choices aligned with our fundamental beliefs about what is meaningful and important.

However, the relationship between identity and decision-making is not always harmonious. The presence of limiting beliefs can cast shadows over this dance, distorting our perceptions and influencing the choices we make. Limiting beliefs, often ingrained during early experiences, act as filters that shape our understanding of ourselves and the world. These beliefs can create self-imposed constraints, narrowing the range of options we consider and influencing the direction of our decisions.

For example, an individual with a limiting belief about their own capabilities may shy away from pursuing challenging opportunities, believing themselves inherently inadequate. This interplay between identity and limiting beliefs becomes a pivotal point of exploration in understanding the dynamics of decision-making. By bringing these beliefs into conscious awareness, we can navigate the path toward more intentional and empowering choices.

Cultivating a positive and empowering self-identity becomes a transformative force in reshaping the relationship between identity and decision-making. This involves a deliberate exploration of the narratives we tell ourselves about who we are and what we are capable of achieving. By fostering self-awareness and challenging self-limiting beliefs, we open the door to a more expansive and resilient self-identity. A positive self-identity acts as a catalyst for confident and aligned decision-making. When individuals perceive themselves as capable, worthy, and adaptable, they are more likely to approach decisions with a sense of agency and optimism. This shift in self-perception creates a ripple effect, influencing the considerations, options, and outcomes of the decisions they encounter.

The relationship between identity and decision-making also extends into the social realm. Our sense of belonging, influenced by our identity, plays a crucial role in choices that involve relationships, collaboration, and societal expectations. The need for social acceptance, rooted in our identity, can shape decisions to conform to societal norms or, conversely, to assert individuality in the face of societal expectations. As we navigate this intricate relationship, it becomes evident that identity is not a static construct but a dynamic and evolving force. Life experiences, personal growth, and self-reflection contribute to the continuous unfolding of our identity, influencing the way we approach and navigate decisions.

In exploring the connection between identity and decision-making processes, it is crucial to recognize the role of self-awareness as a guiding lantern on this journey. The more we understand our values, beliefs, and motivations, the better equipped we are to make decisions that align with our authentic selves. Mindfulness practices, introspection, and a commitment to ongoing self-discovery become invaluable tools in fostering this self-awareness. The exploration of the relationship between identity and decision-making unveils a rich and intricate tapestry. Our identity, woven from the threads of personal and collective experiences, serves as the loom upon which choices are crafted. Recognizing the influence of limiting beliefs and consciously cultivating a positive and empowering self-identity become transformative steps in this journey. As we navigate the interplay between who we are and the decisions we make, we unlock the potential for intentional, aligned, and fulfilling choices that resonate with the essence of our true selves.

Identifying Limiting Beliefs and Their Effect on Choices: Unveiling the Chains that Bind

When it comes to human consciousness, beliefs act as the threads that weave the fabric of our perceptions, actions, and, ultimately, the choices we make. While empowering beliefs can propel us towards growth and fulfillment, limiting beliefs can be insidious chains that constrain our potential and shape the course of our lives. This exploration delves into the profound impact of identifying limiting beliefs and understanding how these silent architects influence the choices we encounter on our life's journey.

The Silent Architects: Understanding Limiting Beliefs

Limiting beliefs are often silent architects, constructing the mental frameworks through which we interpret the world and ourselves. These beliefs, ingrained over time through experiences, societal influences, and internalized narratives, create cognitive filters that influence the choices available to us. Identifying these beliefs requires a keen introspective gaze, a willingness to uncover the subtle whispers that may have been shaping our decisions without our conscious awareness.

Common limiting beliefs often revolve around themes of self-worth, competence, deservingness, and fear of failure or rejection. They may manifest as inner voices that echo phrases like

"I'm not good enough," "I don't deserve success," or "I must avoid failure at all costs." These beliefs, although often formed in response to past experiences, have a pervasive impact on the choices we make in the present.

The Ripple Effect: How Limiting Beliefs Shape Choices

The influence of limiting beliefs extends beyond mere mental constructs; it permeates the very fabric of our decision-making processes. These beliefs create a ripple effect, subtly shaping our perceptions, filtering our options, and influencing the actions we take.

For instance, an individual harboring a limiting belief about their worthiness may find themselves consistently choosing paths that do not align with their true aspirations. This belief becomes a self-fulfilling prophecy, steering choices away from opportunities that could lead to personal or professional growth. In the realm of relationships, limiting beliefs about one's desirability can influence the types of connections individuals pursue or avoid, shaping the dynamics of their social interactions.

Limiting beliefs often act as self-imposed constraints, narrowing the scope of possibilities we consider when faced with decisions. They become the silent architects of our comfort zones, discouraging exploration beyond perceived limitations. Identifying these constraints becomes paramount in unlocking the door to a broader range of choices and embracing the potential for growth and fulfillment.

Unmasking the Limiting Beliefs: A Journey of Self-Discovery

The process of identifying limiting beliefs is a journey of self-discovery that requires courage, self-reflection, and a commitment to unmasking the narratives that may be holding us back. It involves peeling back the layers of automatic thoughts, examining the core beliefs that underpin them, and recognizing the emotional responses triggered by these beliefs.

Journaling, introspective exercises, and engaging in open conversations with trusted confidantes are powerful tools in unmasking limiting beliefs. By exploring recurring patterns in thoughts, emotions, and behaviours, individuals can trace these threads back to their origin and unveil the beliefs that have been silently influencing their choices.

Therapeutic modalities, such as cognitive-behavioural therapy (CBT), provide structured frameworks for identifying and challenging limiting beliefs. CBT involves examining the connections between thoughts, feelings, and behaviours, empowering individuals to reevaluate and reframe the beliefs that may be hindering their growth. The guidance of a skilled therapist can offer invaluable insights and support in this transformative process.

The Impact on Choices Across Life Domains

Limiting beliefs cast shadows across various domains of life, influencing choices in relationships, career, personal development, and overall well-being.

In the realm of relationships, limiting beliefs about trust, vulnerability, or one's inherent worthiness can shape the types of connections individuals pursue or avoid. These beliefs become the silent architects of relationship dynamics, influencing communication patterns, and affecting the quality of connections.

Career choices are profoundly impacted by limiting beliefs around one's competence, potential for success, or fear of failure. Individuals holding limiting beliefs may shy away from challenging opportunities, settle for unfulfilling roles, or hesitate to pursue their true passions. The impact extends beyond professional domains, affecting personal development choices such as education, skill-building, and self-improvement.

Limiting beliefs can also influence choices related to health and well-being. Beliefs about one's ability to adopt healthier habits, overcome challenges, or maintain a positive self-image can shape decisions around diet, exercise, and overall lifestyle. These beliefs contribute to the formation of habits that either support or hinder well-being.

Breaking Free: Challenging and Reframing Limiting Beliefs

Identifying limiting beliefs is a crucial step, but the journey toward empowerment doesn't end there. Breaking free from the chains of these beliefs involves challenging and reframing them, creating mental shifts that open the door to new possibilities.

One effective strategy is to engage in cognitive restructuring, a process that involves consciously challenging and changing negative thought patterns. This entails questioning the validity of limiting beliefs, seeking evidence to the contrary, and actively replacing unhelpful thoughts with more empowering alternatives. The goal is to shift the narrative from one of constriction to one of expansion.

Affirmations and positive self-talk become powerful allies in this process. By consistently reinforcing positive beliefs about oneself, individuals can gradually reshape the mental landscape, fostering a more positive and empowering self-concept. Affirmations serve as daily reminders of the desired beliefs, helping to counteract the influence of limiting thoughts.

Engaging in exposure and behavioural experiments is another effective approach. By deliberately confronting situations that trigger limiting beliefs and challenging oneself to take small, manageable steps outside the comfort zone, individuals can build evidence of their capabilities and resilience. These experiences become counter-narratives that contribute to the reframing of limiting beliefs.

Therapeutic interventions, particularly those rooted in cognitive-behavioural approaches, provide structured frameworks for challenging and reframing limiting beliefs. Working with a therapist allows individuals to explore the origins of these beliefs, understand their impact on choices, and collaboratively develop strategies for change.

Cultivating a Positive and Empowering Self-Identity: The Art of Self-Transformation

In the vast landscape of personal growth and self-discovery, the cultivation of a positive and empowering self-identity emerges as a transformative journey. This exploration delves into the profound impact of how we perceive ourselves and the intentional steps one can take to foster a self-concept that serves as a foundation for fulfillment, resilience, and aligned decision-making.

The Essence of Self-Identity: A Mirror to the Soul

Self-identity serves as a mirror reflecting the essence of who we are — a dynamic interplay of experiences, beliefs, and perceptions that shape our understanding of ourselves. A positive and empowering self-identity is not a static construct but an evolving narrative that influences how we navigate the complexities of life. It forms the cornerstone of our mental and emotional well-being, impacting the choices we make, the relationships we form, and the paths we traverse.

Understanding the components of self-identity involves exploring both the conscious and subconscious layers of our self-concept. Conscious aspects encompass how we view our abilities, qualities, and roles in various life domains. Subconscious elements, on the other hand, often involve deeply ingrained beliefs formed during early experiences that shape our self-worth, competence, and overall sense of deservingness.

The Seeds of Self-Perception: Nurturing Positive Beliefs

The journey towards cultivating a positive and empowering self-identity begins with sowing seeds of positive beliefs about oneself. These beliefs act as the foundation upon which a resilient and uplifting self-concept can grow. Identifying and challenging self-limiting beliefs, often rooted in past experiences or external influences, becomes a crucial initial step.

Positive affirmations, when consistently integrated into daily life, serve as potent tools for nurturing positive self-beliefs. Affirmations are concise, positive statements that reflect desired aspects of oneself. Through repetition, they create a mental environment that supports the development of a constructive self-identity. For example, affirmations such as "I am capable," "I deserve success," or "I am worthy of love" become mantras that counteract negative self-talk and gradually shape a positive self-narrative.

Engaging in self-reflection becomes a mirror to the subconscious layers of self-identity. Exploring the origins of beliefs and challenging those that do not align with one's authentic self allows for a deeper understanding of the intricacies shaping self-perception. Journaling, introspective exercises, and open conversations with trusted confidantes serve as pathways to uncovering and reshaping these foundational beliefs.

The Impact of Positive Self-Identity on Decision Making

The influence of self-identity extends into the realm of decision-making, acting as a silent orchestrator that guides the choices we encounter. A positive and empowering self-identity becomes a compass, directing individuals towards decisions aligned with their aspirations, values, and authentic selves. Individuals with a positive self-identity are more likely to approach decisions with a sense of agency, optimism, and a belief in their ability to navigate challenges. This mindset fosters a willingness to explore new opportunities, take calculated risks, and pursue goals that resonate with their true potential.

In contrast, individuals harboring a negative or limiting self-identity may find their decisions clouded by self-doubt, fear of failure, or a sense of unworthiness. These beliefs become barriers that constrict the range of choices considered, hindering personal and professional growth. The impact of self-identity on decision-making becomes particularly evident in moments of challenge or uncertainty. A positive self-identity acts as a reservoir of resilience, empowering individuals to persevere in the face of setbacks, learn from failures, and view challenges as opportunities for growth. It becomes the lens through which individuals interpret obstacles, shaping a mindset that sees setbacks as temporary and surmountable.

Cultivating Resilience: A Pillar of Positive Self-Identity

Resilience, the ability to bounce back from adversity and adapt to challenges, is intrinsically linked to a positive and empowering self-identity. Cultivating resilience involves fostering a mindset that views setbacks not as reflections of inherent shortcomings but as part of the human experience. Individuals with a resilient self-identity are more likely to view challenges as opportunities for learning and growth. They approach difficulties with a belief in their capacity to overcome obstacles, recognizing that setbacks do not define their worth or potential. This resilience becomes a guiding force in decision-making, enabling individuals to make choices that align with long-term goals rather than succumbing to the immediate pressures of adversity.n The cultivation of resilience involves reframing negative self-talk, challenging catastrophic thinking, and viewing failures as stepping stones rather than insurmountable barriers. By integrating these perspectives into the fabric of self-identity, individuals create a mental environment that supports resilience in the face of life's inevitable challenges.

Social Identity: Connections and Influences

Self-identity is not an isolated construct but exists within the context of social relationships and cultural influences. Social identity encompasses the roles we play in various social groups, the labels assigned to us, and the cultural narratives that shape our sense of belonging. Cultivating a positive and empowering social identity involves nurturing connections that align with one's values and aspirations. Healthy relationships that support authenticity, growth, and mutual respect contribute to a positive social identity. Conversely, toxic relationships that undermine self-worth or impose limiting labels can become barriers to cultivating a positive self-concept. Cultural influences also play a significant role in shaping self-identity. Embracing cultural heritage, celebrating diversity, and challenging stereotypes contribute to a positive cultural identity. This process involves recognizing the richness of one's cultural background, fostering a sense of pride, and actively participating in cultural activities that reinforce a positive connection to one's roots.

The Role of Personal Development: A Continuous Journey

Cultivating a positive and empowering self-identity is not a destination but a continuous journey of personal development. This journey involves a commitment to ongoing self-discovery, learning, and intentional growth. Personal development practices, such as ongoing education, skill-building, and exposure to new experiences, contribute to the evolution of self-identity.

Mindfulness and self-awareness practices become integral tools in this journey. By staying attuned to thoughts, emotions, and behaviours, individuals gain insight into the subtle nuances of their self-identity. Mindfulness practices, such as meditation and reflective exercises, provide spaces for self-discovery, allowing individuals to navigate the complexities of their internal landscape. Setting and pursuing meaningful goals becomes a catalyst for positive self-identity. Goals that align with one's values and aspirations create a sense of purpose and accomplishment, reinforcing the belief in one's ability to shape one's destiny. The pursuit of personal growth becomes a testament to the dynamic nature of self-identity, acknowledging that individuals have the agency to evolve and redefine themselves throughout life.

The Artful Tapestry of Self-Transformation

Cultivating a positive and empowering self-identity is an artful process that involves tending to the delicate threads of self-perception. It is a journey of self-discovery, resilience, and intentional growth that shapes the choices we make and the life we lead. As individuals engage in this transformative journey, they contribute not only to their own well-being but also to the collective tapestry of humanity, creating a ripple effect of positivity and empowerment. Embracing the power of self-identity becomes a celebration of authenticity, a recognition of resilience, and an ongoing invitation to craft a life that resonates with the essence of one's true self.

End of Part 1

Part 2

Strategies and Tools for Behavioural Change

Embarking on the transformative journey of personal growth requires more than introspection and awareness—it demands actionable strategies and tools that empower individuals to reshape their behaviour and forge a path towards lasting change. In Part 2 of "Change Your Life in 30 Days: A Guide to Personal Transformation," we delve into the dynamic realm of Strategies and Tools for behavioural Change. This section serves as a roadmap, offering a curated collection of chapters designed to equip you with the practical insights and actionable steps needed to navigate the complexities of behavioural transformation. Each chapter serves as a beacon, guiding you through the intricacies of setting powerful intentions, building new habits, managing resistance, overcoming obstacles, and initiating mindset shifts that form the bedrock of profound and lasting transformation.

The power of intention is the driving force behind meaningful change. In this chapter, we explore the art and science of setting powerful intentions—clear, purposeful statements that become the compass directing your actions and choices. Understanding the importance of intention in driving change lays the foundation for crafting meaningful and achievable goals. Through practical techniques and insightful guidance, you'll learn to articulate your aspirations, align them with your values, and set intentions that propel you towards a transformative journey. Habits are the architects of behaviour, and building new, positive habits is a cornerstone of sustained change. This chapter delves into the science of habit formation, unraveling the intricacies of how habits shape our daily lives. From breaking old habits that no longer serve you to establishing new ones aligned with your goals, you'll discover practical strategies and actionable steps. Creating supportive environments and leveraging the psychological principles of habit formation, this chapter serves as a guide to sculpting the habits that will lead you towards your desired transformation.

Resistance is a natural companion on the journey of change, but understanding how to navigate and overcome it is a key to success. This chapter explores the nuances of resistance, identifying common obstacles that may hinder your progress. Strategies for overcoming setbacks, cultivating resilience, and addressing the underlying causes of resistance are unveiled. By embracing challenges as opportunities for growth, you'll develop the tools needed to persevere in the face of adversity and continue on your transformative path. The lens through which we view the world profoundly influences our behaviour and choices. In this chapter, we explore the role of mindset in behavioural change and unveil techniques for cultivating a growth mindset. Shifting your mindset involves challenging limiting beliefs, embracing a positive outlook, and harnessing the power of self-belief. Through practical exercises and insightful guidance, you'll discover the transformative potential of changing your mindset as a catalyst for behavioural change.

As you navigate through Part 2 of "Change Your Life in 30 Days," envision this section as your toolbox—a collection of instruments carefully chosen to assist you in the process of profound self-transformation. Each chapter serves as a key, unlocking a different facet of your potential and guiding you towards the behavioural changes that align with the life you aspire to lead. It's not just about knowing; it's about doing. Let this section be your companion on the journey, providing the strategies and tools essential for reshaping your behaviour and charting a course towards a more intentional, fulfilling, and transformative existence.

Chapter 5

Setting Powerful Intentions

When you begin your personal transformation, intentions act as the guiding stars that illuminate the path towards profound and meaningful change. "Setting Powerful Intentions" is not merely a step in the process; it is the catalyst that shapes the trajectory of your journey. In this chapter, we venture into the art and science of intention-setting—an exploration that transcends mere goal-setting and delves into the profound realm of purpose and clarity. Keep in mind your "why", why are you doing this, what is the intention behind it. If you have a big enough "why", then the "what" will always find its way.

Intentions are more than resolutions; they are declarations of the life you wish to create, the person you aim to become, and the values that will shape your actions. Unlike goals, which are often outcome-focused, intentions are rooted in the present moment and reflect the essence of who you are and who you aspire to be. They serve as the compass, directing your choices, behaviours, and responses to the myriad situations life presents. This chapter invites you to embark on a journey of self-discovery and intentional living. We will unravel the layers of your desires, values, and aspirations, allowing you to articulate them into powerful and actionable intentions. Through a blend of introspective exercises, practical techniques, and insightful guidance, you will learn to craft intentions that resonate with your authentic self and align with the transformation you seek.

The process of setting powerful intentions involves more than pen and paper; it requires a deep exploration of your inner landscape. We'll delve into the intricacies of clarifying your vision, understanding the why behind your intentions, and ensuring that they authentically reflect your core values. As you navigate this chapter, envision yourself not just as an architect of change but as the conscious creator of your own destiny. Get ready to embrace the transformative potential that lies within the intentional act of setting powerful intentions. It's time to move beyond the surface-level goals and connect with the deeper currents of your aspirations. As you embark on this chapter, envision your intentions as seeds planted in the fertile soil of your consciousness, ready to sprout into the life you envision. Welcome to a chapter that invites you to declare your intentions boldly, infuse them with purpose, and set the stage for a journey of profound personal transformation.

Understanding the Importance of Clear Intentions in Driving Change

In the weave of personal transformation, the role of clear intentions emerges as a guiding thread, winding through the intricate patterns of behaviour and shaping the direction of one's journey. Intentions are not mere whimsical desires; they are the deliberate and conscious declarations that set the tone for the transformative path ahead. To embark on a journey of change without a clear intention is akin to setting sail without a destination. In this exploration, we delve into the profound significance of understanding the importance of clear intentions in driving change and how this deliberate act becomes the compass navigating the seas of transformation.

Clarity as the North Star: Navigating the Transformative Terrain

Imagine standing at the crossroads of change, unsure of which path to take. Without a clear intention, the journey becomes ambiguous, and the destination remains elusive. Clear intentions serve as the North Star, providing a fixed point of reference that guides decision-making, shapes behaviour, and illuminates the path forward. The clarity of intention becomes the beacon that cuts through the fog of uncertainty, allowing individuals to navigate the transformative terrain with purpose and direction. A well-defined intention is akin to programming the coordinates into your internal GPS—it provides a clear roadmap for your actions and choices. Whether the goal is personal growth, a shift in habits, or a change in perspective, a precisely articulated intention acts as the guiding force that keeps you on course. Without this clarity, the journey becomes meandering, and the transformative potential is diluted in the absence of a focused and intentional direction.

The Power of Conscious Choice: Setting the Stage for Change

Clear intentions empower individuals to make conscious choices aligned with their values and aspirations. When intentions are vague or undefined, decisions become reactive, influenced by external circumstances, societal expectations, or fleeting emotions. In contrast, a well-crafted intention invites individuals to step into the role of conscious architects of their lives, making choices that resonate with the vision they have set for themselves.

Consider the difference between saying, "I want to be healthier," and declaring, "I intend to cultivate a lifestyle that supports my physical well-being." The latter not only articulates the desire for health but also sets the stage for intentional choices—choosing nourishing foods, incorporating regular exercise, and prioritizing self-care. The power of conscious choice embedded in clear intentions transforms vague aspirations into actionable steps, creating a foundation for lasting change.

<u>Alignment with Values: The Heartbeat of Clear Intentions</u>

At the core of clear intentions lies a profound alignment with one's values. Intentions that resonate with your authentic self and core values become the heartbeat of meaningful change. When intentions are in harmony with your values, they carry a depth of purpose and authenticity that propels you forward with unwavering commitment. Consider a person who values connection and community. Their intention to foster meaningful relationships becomes a driving force that influences their choices—engaging in social activities, prioritizing quality time with loved ones, and seeking opportunities to contribute to their community. The alignment with values infuses the intention with a sense of purpose, making it a potent force for change that extends beyond surface-level goals.

Clarity as Motivational Fuel: Sustaining Momentum in Change

The journey of transformation is not a sprint but a marathon, and sustaining momentum requires a source of enduring motivation. Clear intentions act as the motivational fuel that propels individuals through the inevitable challenges and setbacks along the way. When intentions are fuzzy or undefined, the initial enthusiasm may wane as the journey unfolds, leading to a loss of motivation and commitment. On the contrary, clear intentions serve as a reservoir of motivation, reminding individuals of the "why" behind their journey. When faced with obstacles, setbacks, or the temptation to revert to old patterns, the clarity of intention becomes the rallying cry that reignites the flame of motivation. It provides a constant reminder of the transformative purpose, reigniting the commitment to change and propelling individuals forward, even when the path becomes arduous.

Harnessing the Power of Visualization: Seeing the Change Unfold

The mind is a powerful tool, and clear intentions provide the raw material for the art of visualization. When intentions are vividly defined, individuals can create mental images of the desired change, seeing it unfold in the theater of their minds. Visualization becomes a powerful tool for reinforcing intentions, as it engages the subconscious mind and aligns it with the conscious desire for change.

Imagine someone with the clear intention of cultivating a more positive mindset. Through visualization, they can picture themselves responding to challenges with resilience, embracing optimism in the face of adversity, and fostering a more positive internal dialogue. This mental rehearsal not only strengthens the neural pathways associated with the desired change but also serves as a compelling motivator, making the envisioned change feel tangible and achievable.

A North Star in Times of Uncertainty: Navigating Challenges

The transformative journey is not immune to challenges, uncertainties, or moments of doubt. In these times, clear intentions act as a North Star—a constant point of reference that provides stability and guidance. When faced with the complexities of change, individuals can turn to their intentions as a compass, recalibrating their course and recommitting to the path they have intentionally chosen. During challenging moments, the clarity of intention serves as an anchor, grounding individuals in their purpose and reminding them of the transformative vision they have set for themselves. This resilience becomes a testament to the power of clear intentions, transforming obstacles into opportunities for growth and fortifying the resolve to persist on the journey of change.

The Ripple Effect of Clear Intentions: Impact on behaviour and Environment

The influence of clear intentions extends beyond individual behaviour—it ripples through one's environment and influences interpersonal dynamics. When intentions are communicated and shared, they create a shared vision within families, teams, or communities. This collective clarity becomes a catalyst for collaborative change, aligning individuals towards a common purpose and fostering a supportive environment for growth.

Consider a workplace where the intention is to cultivate a culture of innovation. When this intention is clearly communicated and embraced by the team, it becomes the driving force behind collaborative efforts, creative problem-solving, and a shared commitment to continuous improvement. The clarity of intention transforms not only individual behaviour but also the collective dynamics within the environment.

Practical Steps for Setting Clear Intentions: Crafting Your North Star

Setting clear intentions is a deliberate and intentional process, requiring introspection, clarity, and a commitment to authenticity. Here are practical steps to guide you in crafting your North Star of change:

Reflect on Your Values: Begin by identifying your core values. What principles, beliefs, and qualities are most important to you? Your intentions should align with these values to create a sense of purpose and authenticity.

Clarify Your Vision: Envision the change you desire with as much detail as possible. What does success look like? How will you feel? What specific behaviours or habits will characterize this change? Clarity in your vision forms the foundation for your intentions.

Articulate Your Intentions: Write down your intentions in clear and concise language. Use affirmative and present-tense statements, as if the change has already begun. For example, instead of saying, "I want to be more mindful," declare, "I am cultivating mindfulness in my daily life."

Connect Emotionally: Attach emotion to your intentions. How will achieving these intentions make you feel? Connecting emotionally enhances the motivational power of your intentions, making them more compelling and meaningful.

Visualize the Journey: Engage in visualization exercises where you vividly imagine the journey of change. Picture yourself embodying the intentions and experiencing the positive outcomes. Visualization reinforces your commitment and makes the change feel attainable.

Communicate Your Intentions: Share your intentions with trusted friends, family, or colleagues. Articulating your intentions not only reinforces your commitment but also creates a supportive network that encourages and holds you accountable.

Review and Revise: Regularly review your intentions, reflecting on your progress and adjusting them as needed. As you evolve on your journey, your intentions may naturally shift. Embrace this evolution and ensure your North Star remains a true reflection of your aspirations.

Celebrate Milestones: Acknowledge and celebrate small victories along the way. Recognizing progress reinforces your commitment and provides positive reinforcement, creating a momentum that propels you towards larger goals.

Understanding the importance of clear intentions in driving change is akin to recognizing the pivotal role of a compass in navigating uncharted waters. Intentions provide the direction, purpose, and motivation needed to embark on a transformative journey with confidence and clarity. They serve as the North Star that guides individuals through the complexities of change, ensuring that each step is intentional, purposeful, and aligned with the vision of the life they desire. As you craft your clear intentions, envision them not just as statements on paper but as a dynamic force that propels you towards the change you seek—one intentional step at a time.

Crafting Meaningful and Achievable Goals: The Art of Intentional Living

In the grand scheme of personal development, goals are the threads that weave intention into action, transforming aspirations into tangible realities. However, the process of goal-setting is an art that extends far beyond creating a checklist. It involves the delicate balance of crafting goals that are not only meaningful but also achievable, forming the bedrock of intentional living. In this exploration, we delve into the intricacies of this art, unraveling the principles that guide the crafting of goals that resonate with one's aspirations and pave the way for a transformative journey.

Meaningful goals are not arbitrary objectives set in isolation; they are interconnected with one's overarching purpose and values. Before embarking on the journey of goal-setting, it's essential to reflect on the deeper motivations and values that guide your life. What matters to you at a fundamental level? What aspirations align with your authentic self? Crafting meaningful goals involves aligning them with your purpose and values. For instance, if fostering connection and relationships is a core value, a meaningful goal might involve regularly spending quality time with loved ones, initiating conversations, or strengthening existing bonds. These goals derive their significance from their alignment with the values that bring meaning to your life.

Meaningful goals, while inspiring, need to be translated into tangible actions. This is where the importance of clarity and specificity comes to the forefront. Vague or ambiguous goals make it challenging to outline concrete steps and measure progress. Achievability is closely tied to the ability to define your goals with clarity and specificity.

Consider the difference between a vague goal such as "improve my health" and a specific, clear goal like "exercise for 30 minutes at least three times a week." The latter provides a clear roadmap, outlining the specific action, frequency, and duration. Clarity in your goals not only makes them more achievable but also facilitates a focused and intentional approach to the steps needed for success.

SMART Criteria: A Framework for Achievable Goals

To enhance the achievability of goals, the SMART criteria offer a practical framework. SMART stands for Specific, Measurable, Achievable, Relevant, and Time-bound. This framework provides a set of criteria that guide the formulation of goals in a way that enhances clarity and attainability.

Specific: Clearly define what you want to achieve. The more specific your goal, the easier it is to understand and work towards. Ask yourself: What exactly do I want to accomplish?

Measurable: Establish criteria for tracking progress and determining when the goal is achieved. Measurable goals provide a tangible way to assess your journey. Ask yourself: How will I measure my progress?

Achievable: Ensure that your goal is realistic and attainable. While it's admirable to aim high, setting goals that are too lofty can lead to frustration. Ask yourself: Is this goal reasonable and within reach?

Relevant: Align your goal with your overall aspirations and values. Ensure that your goal contributes to your broader sense of purpose. Ask yourself: Does this goal matter to me and align with my values?

Time-bound: Set a timeframe for achieving your goal. This creates a sense of urgency and helps prevent procrastination. Ask yourself: By when do I want to achieve this goal?

Applying the SMART criteria transforms abstract aspirations into actionable goals, enhancing their achievability and providing a structured approach to the pursuit of intentional living.

Breaking Down Goals: From Overwhelming to Attainable Steps

Meaningful and achievable goals often involve breaking down larger aspirations into smaller, manageable steps. The journey of personal transformation is a series of intentional steps, each contributing to the realization of the broader goal. Breaking down goals into smaller components not only makes the process more manageable but also enhances the sense of progress and accomplishment along the way.

For example, if the overarching goal is to write a book, breaking it down into smaller tasks like outlining chapters, setting daily word count goals, and scheduling dedicated writing time transforms a monumental task into a series of achievable steps. Each small step contributes to the larger goal, creating a sense of momentum and success. Life is dynamic, and so too are the circumstances surrounding goal pursuit. Crafting achievable goals requires an understanding of the fluid nature of life and a willingness to adapt. The ability to adjust goals based on changing circumstances or evolving priorities is a hallmark of intentional living.

Consider a scenario where a goal involves attending a weekly fitness class. Unexpected work commitments or family responsibilities may arise, making it challenging to adhere to the original plan. In such instances, the art of adaptability comes into play. Adjusting the goal to include alternative forms of exercise, such as home workouts or shorter sessions, allows for flexibility without compromising the overall objective.

Crafting achievable goals is not a solitary endeavor. Accountability and support play integral roles in fortifying the foundation of goal attainment. Sharing your goals with trusted friends, family, or colleagues creates a network of accountability. Knowing that others are aware of your aspirations adds a layer of responsibility, motivating you to stay committed to your intentions. Additionally, seeking support from those who share similar goals or have expertise in the areas you are exploring can be invaluable. Whether it's a workout buddy, a mentor, or an online community, the support system you build becomes a source of encouragement, guidance, and shared experiences. The collective energy of a supportive network enhances the achievability of goals and reinforces the intentional living mindset.

The journey of goal pursuit is not linear; it's an iterative process that involves reflection and adjustment. Regularly pausing to reflect on your progress, celebrate achievements, and assess challenges allows for ongoing refinement of your goals. Intentional living is not about rigidly adhering to a predetermined plan but about navigating the dynamic landscape of personal growth with awareness and adaptability. If you encounter unforeseen obstacles or if your priorities shift, don't hesitate to adjust your goals accordingly. The ability to reflect on your journey, acknowledge what is working, and pivot when necessary is a key element in the art of crafting meaningful and achievable goals.

Cultivating Intrinsic Motivation: The Driving Force of Achievable Goals

Achievable goals are not solely reliant on external rewards or recognition; they are fueled by intrinsic motivation—the internal drive that stems from a genuine connection to your aspirations. Cultivating intrinsic motivation involves aligning your goals with your passions, values, and a deep sense of purpose. When a goal resonates with your intrinsic motivation, the pursuit becomes inherently rewarding. The joy derived from the journey, the satisfaction of overcoming challenges, and the personal growth experienced along the way become intrinsic sources of motivation. Cultivating this internal drive transforms the pursuit of goals from a duty to a fulfilling and meaningful journey.

The art of crafting achievable goals involves striking a delicate balance between setting targets that stretch your capabilities and maintaining a sense of realism. Goals that are too ambitious may lead to frustration and burnout, while goals that are too modest may lack the motivational pull needed for sustained effort. Applying the Goldilocks principle—finding the "just right" level of challenge—enables you to set goals that push your boundaries without overwhelming your capacity. This balance ensures that your goals are both meaningful and attainable, creating a dynamic tension that propels you towards intentional living with a sense of purpose and accomplishment.

Crafting meaningful and achievable goals is a symphony—a harmonious blend of purpose, clarity, adaptability, and intrinsic motivation. It is the art of translating intentions into actionable steps that resonate with your values and aspirations. As you embark on the journey of intentional living, let your goals be the melody that guides your transformative path, creating a symphony of growth, fulfillment, and purposeful living. In this symphony, every intentional step contributes to the creation of a life that aligns with the essence of who you are and the aspirations that fuel your journey.

Techniques for Setting Intentions Effectively: A Blueprint for Intentional Living

When it comes to personal transformation, setting intentions serves as the initial brushstroke on the canvas of change. Intentions are not mere wishes; they are the conscious declarations that shape the trajectory of our journey. However, the art of setting intentions effectively involves more than casual affirmations. It requires a deliberate and thoughtful approach, a blueprint for intentional living. In this exploration, we uncover the techniques that breathe life into intentions, transforming them from mere statements into powerful catalysts for meaningful change.

1. Cultivate Self-Awareness: The Foundation of Intentional Living

Effective intention-setting begins with a deep understanding of oneself. Cultivating self-awareness involves exploring your values, desires, and the aspects of your life that yearn for transformation. Take time for introspection, reflecting on what truly matters to you, what brings you joy, and where you envision growth. This foundation of self-awareness provides the fertile ground from which meaningful intentions can sprout. Engage in practices such as mindfulness, journaling, or self-reflection exercises. These activities unveil the layers of your authentic self, allowing you to identify the areas of your life that align with your values and those that beckon for intentional change. As you delve into self-awareness, you lay the groundwork for intentions that resonate with the essence of who you are.

2. Clarify Your Values: The Guiding Stars of Intention

Intentions gain strength and purpose when anchored to your core values. Before setting intentions, clarify the principles that define your life and guide your choices. What matters to you at a fundamental level? Is it connection, growth, contribution, or something else? Aligning your intentions with your values ensures that they reflect the authentic compass of your inner self. For example, if one of your core values is personal growth, an intention related to learning a new skill or cultivating a growth mindset harmonizes with this value. The clarity of your values becomes the guiding star that illuminates the path toward intentions deeply rooted in your authentic self.

3. Craft Positive and Affirmative Statements: The Power of Language

Intentions are not wishful thinking; they are affirmative statements that declare your commitment to change. Craft your intentions using positive language, framing them as if they are already happening. Positive affirmations have a transformative effect on your mindset and serve as the building blocks of intentional living. For instance, instead of saying, "I want to reduce stress," declare, "I am cultivating a sense of calm and resilience in the face of challenges." This shift in language reinforces the proactive nature of your intentions and imbues them with a sense of certainty. Positive and affirmative statements not only shape your mindset but also contribute to the manifestation of your intended change.

4. Focus on the Present Moment: The Power of Now

Effective intention-setting transcends future aspirations; it is rooted in the present moment. Intentions are statements of commitment to live a certain way now, influencing your actions in the present. As you set intentions, bring your awareness to the current moment, acknowledging that change begins in the here and now. Avoid framing intentions in a distant future tense. Instead of saying, "I will be more present in my relationships," declare, "I am fully present and engaged in my relationships now." This shift in temporal focus anchors your intentions in the immediacy of your actions, fostering a sense of urgency and commitment to intentional living in the present.

5. Be Specific and Concrete: The Roadmap to Achievement

Vague intentions often lead to unclear paths. To set intentions effectively, be specific and concrete about what you want to achieve. Specificity transforms broad aspirations into actionable steps, creating a roadmap that guides your journey. For example, instead of setting a general intention to "improve my fitness," specify your goal as "I am committed to jogging for 30 minutes three times a week." The specificity provides clarity on the actions required, making your intentions more achievable and contributing to a sense of accomplishment as you progress along the defined path.

6. Visualize Your Intentions: Imprinting the Mind with Change

Visualization is a potent technique that enhances the effectiveness of intention-setting. Create mental images of your intended change, vividly imagining the desired outcomes. Visualization engages the subconscious mind, imprinting it with the vision of success and creating a powerful motivator for intentional living. Take moments to close your eyes and visualize yourself embodying your intentions. See the positive outcomes, feel the emotions associated with success, and immerse yourself in the experience. This practice not only reinforces your commitment but also aligns your subconscious mind with the intentional change you seek, making it a tangible reality in your mental landscape.

7. Connect Emotionally: The Heartbeat of Intentions

Emotion is the heartbeat of effective intention-setting. Attach genuine emotion to your intentions, infusing them with passion, enthusiasm, and a deep sense of purpose. Emotions provide the fuel that propels you forward on your intentional living journey. Consider the difference between saying, "I want to learn a new language" and declaring, "I am excited and passionate about learning a new language to broaden my horizons and connect with different cultures." The emotional connection elevates your intentions from mere goals to heartfelt aspirations, fostering a reservoir of motivation that sustains you through challenges.

8. Prioritize Intentions: The Art of Selective Focus

In the landscape of intentional living, not all aspects of your life may require immediate attention. Prioritize your intentions by focusing on the areas that align with your current goals, values, and the stage of life you are in. Selective focus ensures that your energy and efforts are directed toward the intentions that matter most at a given time. Avoid overwhelming yourself with an abundance of intentions across various domains. Instead, concentrate on a few key areas that hold significant importance. This selective focus enhances the effectiveness of your intention-setting, allowing you to channel your energy into intentional living with purpose and clarity.

9. Use Affirmation and Mantra Practices: Reinforcing Positive Change

Affirmations and mantras are powerful tools that amplify the impact of your intentions. Create affirmations that encapsulate the essence of your intentions and repeat them regularly. Whether written, spoken, or silently affirmed, these practices reinforce positive change on a subconscious level. Integrate affirmation or mantra practices into your daily routine. Repeat your intentions as a morning ritual, incorporate them into meditation, or use them as positive reminders throughout the day. Consistent repetition establishes new thought patterns, strengthening the neural pathways associated with intentional living.

10. Create a Visual Representation: Manifesting Intentions

Visual cues serve as tangible reminders of your intentions, manifesting them in your physical environment. Create a vision board or use symbolic items that represent your intended change. These visual representations act as daily affirmations, reinforcing your commitment to intentional living.bFor example, if your intention is to cultivate a sense of adventure, include images of places you want to explore or symbols that evoke a spirit of curiosity on your vision board. Place this visual representation in a prominent location where you can see it regularly. The visual cues serve as constant reminders of your intentions, aligning your physical space with your internal aspirations.

11. Regularly Review and Reflect: A Journey of Iteration

Intention-setting is not a one-time event; it's a journey of iteration and refinement. Regularly review and reflect on your intentions, assessing your progress, celebrating achievements, and identifying areas for adjustment. This iterative process ensures that your intentions evolve in alignment with your changing circumstances and aspirations.nSet aside dedicated moments for reflection, perhaps weekly or monthly, to revisit your intentions. Consider what is working well, what challenges you have encountered, and whether your priorities have shifted. This reflective practice allows you to fine-tune your intentions, ensuring that they remain potent forces for intentional living.

The Artistry of Intentional Living

In the artistry of intentional living, the techniques for setting intentions effectively serve as the palette from which the masterpiece of personal transformation emerges. The process involves a delicate dance of self-awareness, language, specificity, emotion, and visualization. As you apply these techniques, let your intentions become not just statements but living forces that guide your daily choices, actions, and the trajectory of your life. Remember that the art of intention-setting is an ongoing practice—an ever-evolving exploration of your authentic self and the intentional life you aspire to lead. In each intentional step, you contribute to the creation of a life that aligns with your values, resonates with your passions, and unfolds as a testament to the artistry of intentional living.

Chapter 6

Building New Habits

In the elaborate web of personal transformation, the art of building new habits emerges as a cornerstone—a potent force that shapes our behaviour, defines our routines, and propels us toward intentional living. This chapter delves into the fascinating realm of habit formation, unraveling the science that underlies our daily rituals and exploring strategies to break free from old habits while nurturing the birth of empowering new ones. As we navigate the science of habit formation, we'll embark on a journey of self-discovery, unlocking the keys to behavioural change and creating supportive environments that foster the growth of intentional habits. The path to intentional living begins with the deliberate cultivation of habits that align with our values and aspirations, and this chapter serves as a guide to navigate this transformative terrain. Let's delve into the intricacies of habits, understanding their impact on behaviour, and unveiling the strategies that pave the way for a habit-rich and intentional life.

The Science of Habit Formation and Its Impact on behaviour:
Unraveling the Neural Tapestry of Routine

In our day to day lives, habits weave the fabric of our routines, shaping the contours of our behaviour and influencing the trajectory of our journey. At the heart of this phenomenon lies the science of habit formation—a captivating exploration of how our brains encode, reinforce, and execute routine behaviours. Understanding the intricacies of habit formation not only unveils the neural tapestry that underlies our habits but also empowers us to navigate intentional living by shaping habits that align with our aspirations. At the core of habit formation is a neurological process known as the habit loop, a concept popularized by Charles Duhigg in his book "The Power of Habit." The habit loop comprises three key components: cue, routine, and reward. Understanding this loop provides a window into the neurological underpinnings of our habitual behaviours.

1. Cue: Habits often begin with a cue—a trigger that initiates the behaviour. Cues can be external stimuli, internal emotions, specific times of day, or even the company of certain people. The cue serves as the signal for the brain to engage in the habitual routine.

2. Routine: The routine is the habitual behaviour itself, the action or series of actions that follow the cue. This is the part of the habit loop that is observable in our daily lives, whether it's reaching for a snack when feeling stressed or scrolling through social media at a specific time each day.

3. Reward: The reward is the positive reinforcement that follows the routine. It is the aspect of the habit loop that reinforces the likelihood of repeating the behaviour in the future. Rewards can be physical, emotional, or psychological, providing a sense of pleasure or satisfaction.

Understanding the habit loop is akin to deciphering the code embedded in our daily actions. As we navigate the loop, our brains form neural connections, creating a pathway that facilitates the automatic execution of the routine in response to the cue. Over time, this loop becomes increasingly efficient, transforming the behaviour into a habit that requires minimal conscious effort.

Central to the science of habit formation is the concept of neuroplasticity—the brain's remarkable ability to reorganize itself by forming new neural connections throughout life. Neuroplasticity is the sculptor that molds our brains in response to repeated experiences and behaviours, laying the foundation for the formation of habits. When we engage in a habit consistently, whether it's practicing a musical instrument, exercising, or reading before bed, our brains undergo changes. Neurons that fire together wire together, strengthening the connections associated with the habit loop. Over time, this rewiring makes the habit more automatic and ingrained, a testament to the adaptability of our brains.

The neural orchestration of habit formation involves key regions of the brain, with the basal ganglia and striatum playing pivotal roles. The basal ganglia, a group of nuclei deep within the brain, is responsible for motor control, procedural learning, and the execution of habitual behaviours. The striatum, a component of the basal ganglia, serves as the input center for information related to habits. As we repeat a behaviour within the habit loop, the basal ganglia and striatum work in tandem to encode the sequence of actions and the associated rewards. The more frequently the loop is activated, the more streamlined and automatic the process becomes. This neural efficiency is what transforms a conscious behaviour into a habit etched into the neural landscape of our brains.

The ubiquity of habit loops in our daily lives is astonishing. From the seemingly mundane rituals of morning routines to the intricate dance of decision-making at work, habit loops shape the contours of our existence. However, their impact extends beyond the realm of the routine; habits play a profound role in shaping our character, influencing our well-being, and steering us toward intentional living. Consider the habit loop associated with a daily exercise routine. The cue might be setting out workout clothes, the routine involves engaging in physical activity, and the reward could be the release of endorphins and the sense of accomplishment. Over time, this habit loop not only contributes to physical fitness but also fosters a positive mindset and a commitment to overall well-being.

On a broader scale, the habit loops embedded in our decision-making processes at work, relationships, and personal development significantly influence the course of our lives. Identifying and understanding these habit loops allows us to intentionally shape our behaviours, cultivating habits that align with our values and aspirations.

Breaking Bad Habits: The Power of Awareness and Replacement

While habits often serve as the architects of routine, not all habits contribute positively to our well-being. Breaking bad habits involves a conscious effort to disrupt the habit loop and replace undesirable routines with more constructive behaviours. The power of awareness becomes a potent tool in this process.

Firstly, cultivating awareness of the cue that triggers the unwanted habit is essential. Identifying the circumstances, emotions, or environments that prompt the behaviour allows us to interrupt the habit loop at its inception. This heightened awareness serves as the catalyst for intentional change, creating a mental space for choice and redirection.

Secondly, replacing the routine with a more positive behaviour is crucial. Instead of merely trying to eliminate a habit, focus on substituting it with a healthier alternative. For instance, if the habit involves reaching for a sugary snack when stressed, consider replacing it with a brief mindfulness practice, a short walk, or a healthier snack option. The key is to fill the void left by the old habit with a behaviour that aligns with your well-being goals.

Establishing New Habits: Strategies for Intentional Living

While breaking bad habits requires awareness and replacement, establishing new habits involves intentional cultivation and reinforcement. Here are strategies to foster the creation of intentional habits that contribute positively to your life:

1. Start Small: Micro-Habits for Macro Change

   Begin with small, manageable actions that align with your larger goals. Micro-habits serve as entry points into the habit loop, making the initiation of a new routine less daunting. As these micro-habits become ingrained, they can gradually evolve into more substantial behaviours.

2. Anchor to Existing Habits: Leverage Habit Cues

   Integrate new habits into your existing routines by anchoring them to established habits. Leveraging existing cues makes it easier for the brain to adopt and adapt to the new behaviour. For example, if you want to incorporate a daily stretching routine, anchor it to your morning coffee or evening wind-down.

3. Establish a Trigger: Make the Cue Explicit

   Create a specific trigger or cue that signals the initiation of the new habit. This explicit cue serves as a mental prompt, signaling the brain to engage in the intended behaviour. Whether it's setting a reminder, using a visual cue, or associating the habit with a specific time, establishing a trigger enhances habit consistency.

4. Celebrate Small Wins: Reinforce Positive behaviour

   Acknowledge and celebrate small victories along the way. Recognizing progress reinforces the positive neural connections associated with the habit loop, making the behaviour more likely to repeat. Celebrating milestones, no matter how minor, contributes to the ongoing reinforcement of intentional habits.

5. Create a Supportive Environment: Shape Your Space

    Craft an environment that supports the intended behaviour. Whether it's organizing your workspace for productivity, setting out workout gear for exercise, or creating a designated reading nook for daily learning, a supportive environment enhances the likelihood of habit formation.

6. Utilize Technology: Leverage Tools for Reminders

    Leverage technology to reinforce habit consistency. Set reminders on your phone, use habit-tracking apps, or incorporate wearable devices to prompt and track your progress. Technology serves as a valuable ally in the establishment and maintenance of intentional habits.

7. Practice Mindfulness: Cultivate Present-Moment Awareness

    Integrate mindfulness practices into your daily routine. Mindfulness enhances awareness of your habits, thoughts, and emotions, creating a conscious space for intentional living. Whether through meditation, mindful eating, or breath awareness, cultivating mindfulness supports the intentional formation of habits.

Crafting the Symphony of Intentional Habits

By intentionally living, habits resonate as the instrumental notes that compose the melody of our daily existence. The science of habit formation, rooted in the neural intricacies of the brain, illuminates the pathways through which routines shape our behaviours. By understanding the habit loop, harnessing neuroplasticity, and employing strategies for intentional living, we become the conductors of our habits, orchestrating a symphony that aligns with our values, aspirations, and the intentional life we seek to lead. Through the conscious cultivation of habits, we craft the soundtrack of our lives, creating harmonies that resonate with purpose, well-being, and the ongoing journey of intentional living.

Strategies for Breaking Old Habits and Establishing New Ones: Unraveling the Threads of Transformation

In the intricate tapestry of personal transformation, the endeavor to break old habits and establish new ones unfolds as a nuanced and transformative journey. Whether it's shedding the weight of detrimental routines or sculpting empowering behaviours, the process requires a deliberate orchestration of strategies that address the complexities of habit change. This exploration delves into the art and science of navigating the terrain of breaking old habits and weaving intentional new ones, unraveling the threads of transformation that lead to a life aligned with our values and aspirations.

Before embarking on the journey of habit transformation, it's essential to understand the intricate anatomy of habits. As we've explored in the science of habit formation, habits consist of a loop comprising cue, routine, and reward. Breaking old habits involves disrupting this loop, while establishing new ones requires consciously crafting and reinforcing the habit loop. This understanding serves as the compass that guides our strategies for change.

Strategies for Breaking Old Habits: Liberation from Unwanted Routines

1. Cultivate Awareness: The Power of Mindful Recognition

    Breaking old habits commences with cultivating awareness of the habit loop—recognizing the cues, routines, and rewards associated with the unwanted behaviour. Mindful recognition provides the clarity needed to interrupt the automaticity of the habit loop and opens the doorway to intentional choice.

2. Identify Triggers: Unveiling the Catalysts

    Unveil the triggers or cues that initiate the old habit. Whether it's stress, boredom, specific environments, or emotional states, identifying the catalysts provides insights into the underlying motivations of the habit. Understanding triggers is pivotal for addressing the root causes of the behaviour.

3. Replace with Positive Alternatives: Substitution for Transformation

Breaking old habits is not merely about cessation; it's about replacing the undesirable routine with a positive alternative. Substitute the old behaviour with a constructive action that aligns with your values and well-being goals. This replacement not only disrupts the old habit loop but also introduces a new, intentional routine.

4. Utilize Cognitive behavioural Techniques: Restructuring Thought Patterns

   Cognitive behavioural Therapy (CBT) techniques are powerful tools for habit change. Challenge and restructure the thought patterns associated with the old habit. Identify and modify the irrational beliefs that support the unwanted behaviour, paving the way for cognitive restructuring and behavioural transformation.

5. Set Clear Boundaries: Defining Limitations

   Establish clear boundaries that delineate the limits of the old habit. Define when, where, and under what circumstances the habit is unacceptable. Setting explicit boundaries creates a framework for intentional living, providing a structure that supports the process of breaking free from the old routine.

6. Seek Support: The Strength of Connection

   Breaking old habits can be challenging, and seeking support enhances resilience. Share your goals with friends, family, or a support group. The strength of connection provides encouragement, accountability, and a sense of community that bolsters your efforts in overcoming old habits.

7. Mindfulness and Self-Reflection: The Mirror of Conscious Choice

   Integrate mindfulness and self-reflection practices into your journey of habit change. Cultivate present-moment awareness to observe the impulses and thought patterns associated with the old habit. The mirror of consciousness becomes a tool for making intentional choices in alignment with your desired change.

8. Celebrate Progress: Acknowledging Victories

   Acknowledge and celebrate progress, no matter how small. Breaking old habits is a gradual process, and recognizing victories reinforces the positive neural connections associated with change. Celebrating progress serves as a motivational beacon that lights the path forward.

Strategies for Establishing New Habits: Nurturing the Seeds of Transformation

1. Start Small: Micro-Habits as Catalysts

   Begin the journey of establishing new habits with small, manageable actions. Micro-habits serve as catalysts for change, easing the initiation of a new routine. As these micro-habits become ingrained, they lay the foundation for the cultivation of more substantial behaviours.

2. Anchor to Existing Habits: Leveraging Habit Cues

Integrate new habits into your existing routines by anchoring them to established habits. Leveraging existing cues makes it easier for the brain to adopt and adapt to the new behaviour. For example, if you want to incorporate a daily stretching routine, anchor it to your morning coffee or evening wind-down.

3. Establish a Trigger: Explicit Cue for Intention

Create a specific trigger or cue that signals the initiation of the new habit. This explicit cue serves as a mental prompt, signaling the brain to engage in the intended behaviour. Whether it's setting a reminder, using a visual cue, or associating the habit with a specific time, establishing a trigger enhances habit consistency.

4. Build a Supportive Environment: Shaping Your Space

Craft an environment that supports the intended behaviour. Whether it's organizing your workspace for productivity, setting out workout gear for exercise, or creating a designated reading nook for daily learning, a supportive environment enhances the likelihood of habit formation.

5. Utilize Technology: Tools for Reinforcement

Leverage technology to reinforce habit consistency. Set reminders on your phone, use habit-tracking apps, or incorporate wearable devices to prompt and track your progress. Technology serves as a valuable ally in the establishment and maintenance of intentional habits.

6. Practice Consistency: The Rhythm of Routine

    Consistency is the heartbeat of habit formation. Practice the new habit consistently, embedding it into your daily routine. Repetition reinforces the habit loop, making the behaviour increasingly automatic and ingrained. Consistency transforms intentional actions into ingrained habits.

7. Visualize Success: Imprinting the Mind

    Visualization is a powerful tool for habit establishment. Create mental images of yourself engaging in the new habit, vividly imagining the desired outcomes. Visualization engages the subconscious mind, imprinting it with the vision of success and creating a powerful motivator for intentional living.

8. Accountability Partner: Shared Commitment

    Enlist an accountability partner—a friend, family member, or colleague who shares your commitment to establishing the new habit. The shared journey provides mutual support, encouragement, and a sense of accountability that strengthens your resolve.

9. Reflect and Adjust: The Iterative Journey

    Habit formation is an iterative process. Regularly reflect on your progress, assess what is working well, and be open to adjustments. The iterative journey allows you to fine-tune the habit loop, ensuring that the new behaviour aligns with your evolving goals and aspirations.

The Intersection of Breaking Old Habits and Establishing New Ones

The journey of breaking old habits and establishing new ones is not a linear path but an intricate dance of self-discovery and intentional living. At the intersection of releasing unwanted routines and cultivating empowering behaviours lies the essence of personal transformation. It's a process that demands self-compassion, patience, and a commitment to continuous growth. As you navigate this intersection, recognize that habits are not isolated entities but interconnected threads that weave the fabric of your life. Breaking free from old habits involves unraveling these threads, while establishing new ones requires the conscious weaving of intentional patterns. Embrace the art and science of habit change, acknowledging that each intentional choice contributes to the evolving masterpiece of your life. In the symphony of transformation, breaking old habits and establishing new ones are harmonious notes that resonate with the melody of intentional living. Embrace the rhythm of change, honor the complexities of the journey, and celebrate the evolving tapestry that reflects your commitment to a life shaped by conscious choices.

Creating Supportive Environments for Habit Development: Nurturing the Soil for Growth

Habits are the seeds that, when planted in a supportive environment, can blossom into lasting change. The synergy between habits and their surroundings is a delicate dance, where the environment plays a pivotal role in either fostering or hindering the growth of intentional behaviours. This exploration delves into the art and science of creating supportive environments for habit development, recognizing the profound impact of our surroundings on the seeds of change we aim to cultivate. Before delving into strategies for creating supportive environments, it's crucial to grasp the ecology of habits—the dynamic interplay between individuals and their surroundings. Habits do not exist in isolation; they are intricately woven into the fabric of our daily lives, responding to the cues, triggers, and contexts provided by the environment. Recognizing this interdependence is the first step in shaping environments that nurture intentional habits.

Strategies for Creating Supportive Environments: Cultivating Habit-Friendly Spaces

1. Designing Physical Spaces: A Canvas for Habit Formation

    The physical spaces we inhabit act as canvases where the brushstrokes of our habits take shape. Design your physical environment to align with your habit goals. If your aim is to establish a daily reading habit, create a cozy reading nook with comfortable seating, good lighting, and a selection of inspiring books. Tailor your space to invite the behaviour you intend to cultivate.

2. Removing Temptations: Clearing Pathways to Change

The presence of temptations can act as stumbling blocks on the path to habit development. Identify and remove obstacles or distractions that may lead you away from your intended behaviour. Whether it's decluttering your workspace for focus or minimizing access to unhealthy snacks, creating a clear pathway facilitates the ease of habit formation.

3. Cultivating Social Support: The Power of Connection

The social environment is a potent influencer in habit development. Surround yourself with individuals who support and share your habit goals. Whether it's a workout buddy, a study group, or a reading club, the power of social support enhances motivation, accountability, and a sense of shared commitment. Cultivating a positive social environment acts as a fertile ground for habit growth.

4. Establishing Rituals and Cues: Synchronizing Habit Triggers

Integrate intentional cues and rituals into your environment to signal the initiation of the desired behaviour. Whether it's setting out your workout clothes the night before, placing a book on your bedside table for nightly reading, or creating a dedicated workspace for focused tasks, establishing clear cues synchronizes your environment with the rhythm of habit development.

5. Utilizing Technology: Tools for Reinforcement

    Leverage technology to reinforce supportive environments. Set reminders on your phone, use habit-tracking apps, or incorporate wearable devices to prompt and track your progress. Technology serves as a valuable ally in shaping environments that reinforce intentional habits, providing real-time feedback and nudges toward positive behaviours.

6. Creating Visual Reminders: Anchors for Intention

    Visual cues serve as powerful anchors that remind us of our intentions. Create visual reminders in your environment that represent your habit goals. Whether it's a vision board, sticky notes with affirmations, or symbolic items that evoke the desired behaviour, these visual anchors act as constant nudges, reinforcing your commitment to intentional habits.

7. Aligning Habits with Values: Integrity in Environment

    Ensure that your environment aligns with your core values and aspirations. When your habits are in harmony with your values, the environment becomes a reflection of your authentic self. Aligning habits with values creates an environment that fosters a sense of integrity and purpose, reinforcing the meaningfulness of the behaviours you aim to cultivate.

8. Adapting to Change: Dynamic Environments for Growth

   Recognize that environments are not static; they evolve with time and circumstances. Adaptability is a key element in creating supportive environments for habit development. Be willing to reassess and adjust your surroundings as your habits evolve, ensuring that your environment continues to provide the nourishment needed for sustained growth.

The Interplay of Internal and External: Aligning Mind and Environment

Creating supportive environments for habit development is not solely about external factors; it's also about aligning the mind with the surroundings. The interplay between internal motivation and external cues is a dynamic dance that shapes the trajectory of habit growth.

1. Mindful Presence: The Catalyst for Change

   Cultivate mindful presence in your environment. Mindfulness enhances awareness of the present moment, allowing you to consciously engage with your surroundings. Whether it's savoring the aroma of a cup of tea during your reading time or appreciating the natural beauty of your workout space, mindful presence transforms environments into intentional sanctuaries for habit development.

2. Intentional Anchoring: Linking Internal Goals with External Cues

   Anchor your internal goals to external cues in your environment. This intentional linking reinforces the connection between your aspirations and the physical spaces you inhabit. For example, if your goal is to practice gratitude daily, place a gratitude journal in a visible location as a tangible reminder of your internal commitment.

3. Environmental Mindset: Shaping Beliefs about Spaces

Cultivate an environmental mindset that shapes your beliefs about the spaces you occupy. Viewing your environment as a partner in habit development transforms spaces into allies rather than passive backdrops. Consciously shape your beliefs about how your surroundings can contribute to your growth, reinforcing a positive and intentional mindset.

Case Studies in Habit-Optimized Environments: Realizing Potential

The Home Gym Oasis: A Haven for Physical Wellness

Imagine a home gym designed with vibrant colors, ample natural light, and motivational quotes. This environment becomes a haven for physical wellness, eliminating the barriers of commuting to a gym and creating a space where the habit of daily exercise seamlessly integrates into the flow of daily life.

The Productivity Nook: Crafting a Workspace for Focus

Designing a dedicated productivity nook with minimal distractions, ergonomic furniture, and personalized elements can transform the workspace into a hub for focused work. This habit-optimized environment enhances concentration, creativity, and the efficiency of daily tasks.

The Reading Retreat: Curating Spaces for Intellectual Growth

Creating a reading retreat with cozy seating, soft lighting, and shelves of inspiring books transforms the environment into a sanctuary for intellectual growth. This habit-friendly space encourages the habit of daily reading, providing a tranquil haven where the mind can delve into the realms of knowledge and imagination.

Environments as Partners in Growth

With habit development, environments emerge as silent yet influential partners, shaping the melodies of our daily lives. Creating supportive environments is an art that involves intentional design, mindful presence, and the alignment of internal aspirations with external cues. As we cultivate habit-friendly spaces, we recognize that our surroundings are not passive spectators but dynamic collaborators in the journey of personal transformation. By weaving the threads of supportive environments into the fabric of our habits, we harness the power of synergy. The dance between internal motivations and external cues becomes harmonious, creating a fertile ground where the seeds of intentional behaviours can take root and flourish. As we navigate the landscapes of habit development, let us embrace the role of environments as nurturing allies, acknowledging their profound impact on the growth, sustainability, and blossoming potential of intentional habits.

Chapter 7

Managing Resistance and Overcoming Obstacles

In the labyrinth of personal transformation, the path to change is often met with the formidable companions of resistance and obstacles. This chapter serves as a guiding light through the twists and turns of navigating challenges, providing insights into managing resistance, overcoming common obstacles, and nurturing the resilience needed to weather the storms of transformation. Recognizing that resistance is a natural response to change, we embark on a journey to understand its nuances, unveiling strategies to dismantle barriers, and forging the inner strength required to persevere in the face of adversity. Resistance, like a shadow cast by the prospect of change, often emerges as a natural echo in the corridors of transformation. It manifests in various forms, from the subtle tug of comfort zones to the overt protests of ingrained habits. Before we delve into strategies for managing resistance, it's crucial to acknowledge its presence and understand the underlying dynamics. Recognizing that resistance is not an adversary but a guidepost illuminates the path to effective change.

The journey of personal transformation is akin to a quest, and quests are seldom without obstacles. This chapter unveils a toolkit of strategies crafted to overcome common obstacles encountered on the path to change. From the boulders of self-doubt to the thorns of procrastination, each obstacle becomes an opportunity for growth. By dissecting these challenges and providing practical approaches, we empower ourselves to navigate the terrain with resilience and determination.

Resilience and perseverance stand as the armor of the change warrior, fortifying the spirit against the uncertainties and tribulations of the transformative journey. This section explores the art of cultivating resilience, weaving a tapestry of inner strength that withstands the tests of time. Through stories of triumph over adversity and practical techniques for bolstering perseverance, we illuminate the path to not only survive challenges but thrive in their midst.

As we embark on Chapter 7, let us embrace the inevitability of resistance and obstacles as integral parts of the change landscape. By understanding their nuances, deploying strategic approaches, and fortifying our inner resolve, we emerge as architects of our destiny, sculpting a path that transcends resistance, overcomes obstacles, and ultimately leads to the transformative destination awaiting us on the other side.

Recognizing and Addressing Resistance to Change: Illuminating the Shadows of Transformation

Change, with its promise of growth and renewal, often encounters a silent adversary in the form of resistance. Like shadows cast by the prospect of transformation, resistance can cloak itself in myriad guises, subtly influencing our thoughts, emotions, and behaviours. In this exploration, we unravel the intricacies of recognizing and addressing resistance to change, understanding it not as an antagonist but as a guidepost illuminating the unexplored territories of our growth journey. Resistance, at its core, is a dance between the comfort of the familiar and the discomfort of the unknown. It thrives in the sanctuary of routines, habits, and familiar landscapes, where the predictable rhythms of life offer a sense of security. The prospect of change disrupts this equilibrium, challenging the status quo and introducing uncertainty. Recognizing resistance begins with acknowledging this dance, understanding that the discomfort it brings is often a signpost pointing toward the uncharted territories of personal growth. Resistance communicates through a language of discontent, manifesting in subtle signs and signals. Recognizing these indicators is the first step in addressing resistance effectively. Common signs include:

1. Procrastination and Avoidance: Procrastination becomes a loyal companion when resistance lurks in the shadows. Delaying actions, avoiding tasks, and finding excuses are ways resistance manifests, creating a buffer against the discomfort of change.
2. Denial and Rationalization: Resistance often wears the mask of denial or rationalization, attempting to convince us that change is unnecessary or that the current state is preferable. Recognizing these rationalizations is essential to confront the underlying resistance.
3. Emotional Reactions: Unexplained emotions such as anxiety, fear, or frustration may signal underlying resistance. These emotional responses act as messengers, revealing areas where the psyche is grappling with the prospect of change.

4. Defensiveness: A defensive stance, whether in personal relationships or professional settings, can be indicative of resistance. The ego, seeking to protect the status quo, may manifest defensiveness as a shield against perceived threats.
5. Seeking External Validation: Constantly seeking external validation or approval may be a manifestation of resistance. The reluctance to trust one's instincts and decisions can stem from the fear of venturing into unknown territory.

<u>Exploring the Roots of Resistance</u>

Unveiling the Unconscious Forces. Resistance often conceals its roots in the depths of the unconscious mind. Exploring these roots requires a willingness to delve into the recesses of our thoughts, beliefs, and past experiences. Key factors contributing to resistance include:

1. Fear of the Unknown: The uncertainty accompanying change triggers the primal fear of the unknown. Resistance may manifest as a defense mechanism against the perceived risks and uncertainties associated with unfamiliar territory.
2. Loss of Control: Change implies a shift in the locus of control, and this loss of control can be unsettling. Resistance may emerge as an attempt to maintain a sense of autonomy and predictability in the face of impending change.
3. Comfort Zone Dynamics: The comfort zone, while providing a sense of security, can also become a breeding ground for resistance. Breaking away from the familiar requires stepping beyond the confines of the comfort zone, and resistance may emerge as a defense of the status quo.
4. Past Traumas and Failures: Unresolved past traumas or failures can cast a long shadow on the willingness to embrace change. Resistance may be rooted in the fear of repeating past mistakes or facing similar challenges.

Strategies for Addressing Resistance: A Compass for Change

Addressing resistance requires a nuanced approach that combines self-awareness, empathy, and strategic interventions. Here are effective strategies for navigating the complexities of resistance:

Cultivate Self-Awareness: The journey of addressing resistance begins with self-awareness. Reflect on your thoughts, emotions, and behaviours to identify signs of resistance. Journaling, mindfulness practices, and regular introspection serve as tools for cultivating self-awareness.

Empathetic Inquiry: Approach resistance with empathy, recognizing it as a legitimate response to change. Engage in empathetic inquiry, asking yourself or others about the specific fears, concerns, or discomfort associated with the impending change. Creating a safe space for open communication fosters understanding and trust.

Break Down Change into Manageable Steps: Overwhelming change can amplify resistance. Break down the change into smaller, manageable steps. By focusing on incremental progress, you make the path less intimidating and more achievable, mitigating resistance along the way.

Communicate Transparently: Transparent communication is a powerful antidote to resistance. Clearly articulate the reasons for change, the expected benefits, and the support available.

Transparency builds trust and reduces uncertainty, addressing the fear of the unknown.

Highlight the Benefits: Emphasize the positive outcomes and benefits associated with the change. By painting a vivid picture of the rewards and growth opportunities, you shift the focus from discomfort to the potential for personal and collective advancement.

Offer Support and Resources: Resistance often stems from the perceived lack of resources or support. Ensure that individuals undergoing change have the necessary tools, training, and support systems. Addressing practical concerns contributes to a sense of preparedness and reduces resistance.

Create a Collaborative Environment: Involve individuals in the change process, creating a collaborative environment where their input is valued. When people feel included in decision-making and have a sense of ownership, resistance diminishes, and a collective commitment to change emerges.

Provide a Vision of the Future: Paint a compelling vision of the future that resonates with individuals. A clear and inspiring vision serves as a beacon, guiding individuals through the discomfort of change toward a destination that aligns with their values and aspirations.

<u>Case Studies in Addressing Resistance: Lessons from the Frontlines</u>

Organizational Restructuring: In the context of organizational restructuring, employees may resist changes in job roles or reporting structures. Transparent communication about the reasons for the restructuring, opportunities for skill development, and support in the transition process can effectively address resistance.

Adopting Healthy Habits: On a personal level, resistance to adopting healthy habits may manifest in procrastination or rationalization. Breaking down the habit change into manageable steps, understanding the underlying fears of failure or discomfort, and creating a supportive environment can address resistance and pave the way for lasting change.

Technological Upgrades: Technological upgrades within a company can be met with resistance due to concerns about adaptability and the perceived disruption to daily workflows. In such cases, providing comprehensive training, creating a support system for troubleshooting, and highlighting the long-term efficiency gains can address resistance.

Transforming Resistance into Catalyst for Growth

In the tapestry of personal and organizational change, resistance is not a roadblock but a dynamic force that, when understood and addressed, can become a catalyst for growth. By recognizing the signs, exploring the roots, and deploying strategic interventions, we transform resistance from an adversary into a guidepost pointing toward unexplored realms of potential. As we navigate the shadows of resistance, let us embrace the discomfort as an integral part of the change journey. In doing so, we not only dismantle barriers to transformation but also cultivate a resilient spirit capable of navigating the ever-evolving landscapes of personal and collective growth.

The journey of personal transformation is a dynamic landscape marked by peaks of triumphs and valleys of challenges. Setbacks and obstacles, though inevitable, need not be roadblocks; instead, they can serve as stepping stones for growth. This exploration delves into the strategies crafted to overcome common obstacles and setbacks, offering a compass to navigate the rugged terrains of change and emerge stronger on the other side.

Understanding the Nature of Obstacles: Mapping the Topography of Challenges

Obstacles, like the twists and turns of a winding path, come in various forms. Whether it's a sudden detour, a steep incline, or a momentary pause, each obstacle carries the potential to test our resolve and resilience. Recognizing the common types of obstacles is the first step in crafting strategies to overcome them:

Internal Resistance: Internal resistance emerges from within, often in the form of self-doubt, fear, or ingrained habits that resist change. Overcoming internal resistance requires introspection, self-compassion, and a commitment to challenging limiting beliefs.

External Challenges: External challenges encompass factors beyond individual control, such as changes in the external environment, unexpected events, or societal shifts. Navigating external challenges involves adaptability, strategic planning, and a proactive approach to mitigate their impact.

Lack of Resources: Insufficient resources, whether in the form of time, finances, or support, can pose significant obstacles. Overcoming resource constraints involves creative problem-solving, prioritization, and leveraging available resources effectively.

Fear of Failure: The fear of failure can immobilize progress, leading to procrastination or hesitancy. Overcoming the fear of failure requires reframing perspectives, viewing mistakes as opportunities for learning, and fostering a growth mindset.

Setbacks and Plateaus: Setbacks and plateaus are natural phases in any transformation journey. Overcoming these periods involves resilience, patience, and a strategic reassessment of goals and approaches.

Strategies for Overcoming Obstacles: A Toolkit for Triumph

Mindful Awareness: Cultivate mindful awareness to recognize obstacles as they arise. Mindfulness allows you to observe thoughts and emotions without judgment, creating space for intentional responses rather than reactive behaviours. Regular mindfulness practices, such as meditation or deep breathing, enhance self-awareness and emotional regulation.

Goal Refinement: When faced with obstacles, revisit and refine your goals. Break down larger objectives into smaller, achievable steps. By focusing on incremental progress, you maintain momentum and build a sense of accomplishment, even in the face of challenges.

Adaptability and Flexibility: Embrace adaptability as a cornerstone of overcoming obstacles. Life is inherently unpredictable, and the ability to adjust course in response to changing circumstances is a valuable skill. Cultivate flexibility in both mindset and strategies, allowing for adjustments as needed.

Strategic Planning: Develop strategic plans that anticipate potential obstacles. Identify contingency measures and alternative pathways to circumvent challenges. A well-thought-out plan provides a roadmap for navigating obstacles, minimizing disruptions to progress.

Seeking Support: Reach out for support when facing obstacles. Whether it's seeking guidance from mentors, collaborating with peers, or sharing concerns with friends and family, a support network provides valuable perspectives, encouragement, and practical assistance.

Learning from Setbacks: View setbacks as opportunities for learning and growth. Analyze the factors contributing to setbacks, extract lessons, and apply newfound insights to future endeavors. Adopting a growth mindset transforms setbacks into stepping stones for continuous improvement.

Cultivating Resilience: Cultivate resilience as a core attribute for overcoming obstacles. Resilience involves bouncing back from setbacks, maintaining a positive outlook, and adapting to adversity. Develop resilience through practices such as building a strong support network, fostering optimism, and nurturing self-care habits.

Time Management: Efficient time management is crucial for navigating obstacles. Prioritize tasks based on importance and urgency, allocate dedicated time for focused work, and set realistic deadlines. Effective time management ensures that setbacks do not lead to a cascade of unmet deadlines.

Celebrate Small Wins: Celebrate small victories along the way. Acknowledge and celebrate achievements, no matter how modest, to reinforce a positive mindset. Recognizing progress, even in the face of obstacles, boosts motivation and resilience.

Adopting a Growth Mindset: Embrace a growth mindset that views challenges as opportunities for learning and improvement. A growth mindset fosters a belief in the capacity for change and resilience in the face of setbacks. Challenge fixed beliefs about capabilities and embrace the potential for ongoing development.

Case Studies in Overcoming Obstacles: Narratives of Triumph

Career Transition Challenges:

Imagine an individual navigating a career transition, facing uncertainties and doubts about the new path. By seeking guidance from mentors, breaking down the transition into manageable steps, and viewing setbacks as opportunities to refine goals, this individual successfully overcomes obstacles and builds a fulfilling career in a new field.

Fitness Journey Setbacks:

In the context of a fitness journey, setbacks such as injuries or plateaus can be disheartening. By adapting workout routines to accommodate injuries, seeking professional guidance, and viewing plateaus as opportunities to reassess and diversify training methods, an individual transforms setbacks into catalysts for improved fitness and well-being.

Entrepreneurial Ventures:

Consider an entrepreneur facing challenges in a competitive market. Through strategic planning, adaptability to market dynamics, seeking mentorship from experienced entrepreneurs, and maintaining a resilient mindset, this entrepreneur navigates obstacles, refines business strategies, and achieves sustainable growth.

In the labyrinth of transformation, obstacles are not roadblocks but integral features of the journey. By understanding their nature, deploying strategic approaches, and maintaining resilience, individuals can triumph over trials and emerge stronger on the other side. The strategies for overcoming common obstacles and setbacks form a versatile toolkit, equipping individuals to navigate the rugged terrains of change with grace, determination, and an unwavering commitment to their transformative journey.

Cultivating Resilience and Perseverance in the Face of Challenges: The Art of Triumph over Adversity

Life's journey is a tapestry woven with threads of joy, triumph, and, inevitably, challenges. In the face of adversity, the twin virtues of resilience and perseverance emerge as guiding stars, illuminating the path forward. This exploration delves into the art of cultivating resilience and perseverance, not merely as responses to challenges but as transformative forces that empower individuals to navigate the complexities of life with grace and fortitude. Resilience, often likened to the elasticity of a rubber band, signifies the human spirit's capacity to bounce back from setbacks, adapt to change, and withstand the trials of life. It is an inner strength that goes beyond mere endurance, embracing challenges as opportunities for growth. Understanding resilience involves recognizing its multifaceted nature:

Emotional Resilience:

Emotional resilience involves navigating and adapting to emotional challenges. It's the ability to acknowledge and express emotions, regulate emotional responses, and bounce back from setbacks with a renewed sense of purpose and stability.

Cognitive Resilience:

Cognitive resilience pertains to the mental fortitude to face and overcome cognitive challenges. This includes maintaining a positive mindset, adopting a problem-solving approach, and reframing negative thoughts into constructive perspectives.

Social Resilience:

Social resilience encompasses the ability to maintain healthy relationships and seek support during challenging times. Building a strong social support network provides a buffer against the impact of adversity and fosters a sense of connectedness.

Physical Resilience:

Physical resilience involves maintaining physical well-being in the face of challenges. This includes practices such as regular exercise, adequate sleep, and a healthy lifestyle, which contribute to the overall ability to withstand and recover from stressors.

The Role of Perseverance: A Steadfast Commitment to the Journey

While resilience allows individuals to weather the storms, perseverance is the unwavering commitment to continue the journey despite the challenges encountered. Perseverance involves determination, persistence, and a focus on long-term goals, even in the face of obstacles. It's a quality that propels individuals forward when the path seems arduous and the destination distant.

Strategies for Cultivating Resilience: Nurturing the Inner Flame

Developing a Growth Mindset:

Cultivate a growth mindset that sees challenges as opportunities for learning and development. Embrace the belief that abilities can be developed through dedication and hard work, fostering resilience in the face of setbacks.

Building Self-Compassion:

Practice self-compassion by treating oneself with kindness and understanding, especially during difficult times. Self-compassion involves acknowledging one's humanity, embracing imperfections, and offering oneself the same support and encouragement given to others.

Fostering Social Connections:

Cultivate and strengthen social connections. The support of friends, family, and a broader community provides a foundation of resilience. Sharing experiences, seeking advice, and offering support create a web of connections that sustains individuals through challenges.

Practicing Mindfulness and Stress Reduction:

Integrate mindfulness practices into daily life to manage stress and enhance resilience. Mindfulness involves being fully present in the moment, accepting experiences without judgment, and developing a calm awareness that contributes to emotional and mental resilience.

Setting Realistic Goals:

Establish realistic and achievable goals. Setting objectives that align with one's values and capacities allows for a sense of accomplishment, reinforcing the belief in one's ability to overcome challenges.

Strategies for Cultivating Perseverance: Navigating the Long Road Ahead

Clarifying Long-Term Goals:

Define long-term goals with clarity and specificity. Having a clear vision of the desired outcome provides a compass for perseverance, guiding individuals through the inevitable challenges encountered on the journey.

Breaking Down Goals into Milestones:

Break down long-term goals into manageable milestones. Perseverance is sustained by celebrating small victories along the way. Achieving milestones provides a sense of progress and fuels motivation for the next steps.

Maintaining Focus on Intrinsic Motivation:

Connect with intrinsic motivations rather than relying solely on external rewards. Intrinsic motivation, driven by personal values and passions, serves as a deep well of perseverance, ensuring a sustained commitment to the journey irrespective of external circumstances.

Cultivating a Positive Inner Dialogue:

Foster a positive inner dialogue that reinforces perseverance. Replace self-doubt and negative self-talk with affirmations that highlight strengths, past successes, and the potential for growth. A positive inner dialogue serves as a powerful ally on the road to perseverance.

Embracing Adaptability:

Embrace adaptability as a companion to perseverance. The ability to adapt to changing circumstances and adjust strategies when necessary ensures a dynamic and resilient approach to long-term goals. Adaptability allows individuals to navigate detours without losing sight of the destination.

Cultivating resilience and perseverance is akin to composing a symphony of triumph, where each note represents a response to life's challenges and a commitment to the journey ahead. Resilience and perseverance, when harmoniously integrated, form the backbone of a resilient spirit that not only weathers storms but transforms adversity into a catalyst for growth. In the grand tapestry of life, the art of triumph over challenges lies in the dynamic interplay of resilience and perseverance, creating a melody that resonates with the indomitable spirit of the human journey.

Chapter 8

Mindset Shifts for Transformation: A Journey into the Power of Perspective

As we stand on the threshold of the final chapter in Part 2 of our transformative odyssey, we embark on a profound exploration into the intricate landscape of mindset shifts. Chapter 8, "Mindset Shifts for Transformation," is a culmination of our endeavors to understand the profound role that mindset plays in the realm of behavioural change. Here, we unravel the threads of thought that weave the fabric of our beliefs, perceptions, and ultimately, our actions. In this transformative journey, we delve into the core principles that define the landscape of mindset and unearth techniques that empower the cultivation of a growth mindset. With an unwavering focus on harnessing the transformative power of positive thinking and self-belief, this chapter serves as a compass guiding us toward the zenith of personal evolution. Join us as we illuminate the path to profound mindset shifts, unlocking the doors to a future where the power of perspective becomes the driving force behind lasting behavioural transformation.

The Role of Mindset in behavioural Change: Unlocking the Gateway to Transformation

At the heart of every behavioural transformation lies the silent orchestrator of change—the mindset. Chapter 8 invites us to unravel the intricacies of this unseen force, exploring how our beliefs, attitudes, and perceptions shape the trajectory of our behavioural evolution. The role of mindset in behavioural change is not merely incidental; it is the linchpin that holds the entire transformational framework together, dictating the boundaries of what we deem possible and influencing the choices we make on our journey toward personal growth.

Mindset, in its essence, is the lens through which we perceive and interpret the world. It is the sum total of our beliefs, attitudes, and assumptions about ourselves, others, and the circumstances we encounter. In the context of behavioural change, mindset serves as the architect of our belief systems, constructing the foundation upon which our actions and reactions are built.

Fixed vs. Growth Mindset: A fundamental duality within the realm of mindset is the distinction between a fixed mindset and a growth mindset. A fixed mindset operates under the premise that abilities and traits are static, leading individuals to shy away from challenges and view setbacks as indicators of inherent limitations. Conversely, a growth mindset thrives on the belief that abilities can be developed through effort, learning, and perseverance, fostering resilience in the face of challenges.

Limiting Beliefs and Empowering Beliefs: Mindset shapes the beliefs that either confine us within self-imposed limitations or empower us to transcend perceived boundaries. Limiting beliefs, often ingrained from early experiences or societal conditioning, can create mental barriers that impede behavioural change. On the other hand, empowering beliefs open doors to possibilities, instilling confidence and a sense of agency in the change process.

Fixed Identity vs. Evolving Identity: Identity, a cornerstone of mindset, can be viewed as fixed or evolving. A fixed identity rigidly adheres to a set self-concept, resisting change for fear of destabilizing this identity. In contrast, an evolving identity embraces the fluidity of personal growth, recognizing that change is an integral part of the human experience.

The Dynamics of Mindset in behavioural Change: Breaking the Chains of Inertia

Self-Fulfilling Prophecy: The self-fulfilling prophecy, a phenomenon intimately tied to mindset, underscores how our beliefs about ourselves influence our behaviour in a way that aligns with those beliefs. If we perceive ourselves as capable and resilient, our actions tend to manifest those qualities, creating a positive feedback loop of reinforcement.

Motivation and Effort: Mindset significantly influences our motivation and willingness to exert effort in the pursuit of behavioural change. A growth mindset fosters a belief that effort leads to improvement, making individuals more likely to engage in sustained and purposeful efforts to overcome challenges.

Perception of Challenges: The way we perceive challenges is a direct reflection of our mindset. A fixed mindset may view challenges as insurmountable obstacles, triggering avoidance or feelings of helplessness. In contrast, a growth mindset sees challenges as opportunities for learning and growth, encouraging individuals to embrace difficulties as stepping stones to success.

Resilience in the Face of Setbacks: Setbacks, inherent in any transformative journey, elicit varied responses based on mindset. A fixed mindset may interpret setbacks as indicators of incompetence, leading to demotivation and a reluctance to persevere. In contrast, a growth mindset views setbacks as temporary hurdles, inspiring resilience, and a commitment to overcoming obstacles.

Harnessing the Power of Positive Thinking and Self-Belief: Illuminating the Path to Transformation

Positive Thinking as a Catalyst: Positive thinking, intertwined with mindset, acts as a catalyst for behavioural change. Cultivate optimistic and constructive thoughts that reinforce the belief in one's ability to navigate challenges and achieve desired outcomes. Positive thinking serves as a powerful force in shaping attitudes and influencing behaviour.

Affirmations and Self-Belief: Affirmations, positive statements that reinforce desired beliefs, play a pivotal role in building self-belief. Create and recite affirmations that align with the behavioural change objectives, fostering a positive self-concept and bolstering confidence in the ability to achieve transformation.

Visualization for Success: Visualization, a technique rooted in positive psychology, involves mentally picturing successful outcomes. By vividly imagining the attainment of behavioural change goals, individuals enhance self-belief, create a mental blueprint for success, and cultivate a positive expectancy for the future.

In the crucible of behavioural change, mindset emerges as the alchemist that transmutes beliefs into actions and intentions into realities. The role of mindset in behavioural change is not confined to mere perception; it is the fulcrum upon which the lever of transformation pivots. As we navigate the landscapes of personal evolution, let us recognize the potency of mindset—whether fixed or growth—in shaping the contours of our transformative journey. Through intentional cultivation, resilience in the face of challenges, and the harnessing of positive thinking and self-belief, we unlock the gateway to a future where the power of perspective becomes the driving force behind lasting behavioural change. The canvas of transformation awaits the brushstrokes of a mindset attuned to growth, resilience, and the boundless possibilities that lie ahead.

With personal development, the growth mindset emerges as a resounding melody, harmonizing with the chords of resilience, effort, and the unwavering belief in one's capacity for change. Cultivating a growth mindset is not a mere intellectual exercise; it is a transformative journey that involves reshaping the very fabric of one's beliefs and attitudes toward learning and development. This exploration delves into the techniques that serve as the nurturing soil for the seeds of a growth mindset, empowering individuals to navigate challenges with an open heart and a steadfast commitment to personal evolution.

1. Embrace Challenges as Opportunities: The cornerstone of a growth mindset lies in the ability to view challenges as opportunities for learning and growth. Rather than shying away from difficulties, embrace them as chances to stretch beyond your current capabilities. Develop a mindset that recognizes challenges not as threats to your competence but as stepping stones toward mastery. Each obstacle encountered on the path to personal evolution is an invitation to refine skills, gain new insights, and ultimately expand the boundaries of your potential.

Technique: Challenge Journaling

- *Keep a journal where you document challenges encountered and the lessons learned from each experience.*
- *Reflect on how challenges have contributed to your growth and the skills you've developed along the way.*
- *Set intentional goals to take on new challenges, fostering a proactive approach to continuous learning.*

2. View Effort as the Path to Mastery:

In the realm of a growth mindset, effort is not a sign of inadequacy but a testament to the journey toward mastery. Cultivate the belief that sustained effort leads to improvement and that every endeavor contributes to personal development. Rather than viewing challenges through the lens of innate talent, shift the focus to the process of learning and the incremental progress achieved through dedicated effort.

Technique: Effort Recognition

- *Acknowledge and celebrate your own effort, irrespective of the immediate outcome.*

- *Establish a mindset that values the journey of improvement over a fixation on immediate results.*
- *Set specific goals that require consistent effort and perseverance, reinforcing the idea that growth is a continuous process.*

3. Learn from Criticism:

A growth mindset welcomes criticism not as a blow to self-worth but as constructive feedback for improvement. Embrace criticism as an invaluable source of information that can guide your journey toward personal and professional development. Rather than interpreting feedback defensively, approach it with a curious and open mindset, recognizing that it offers insights into areas for refinement and growth.

Technique: Constructive Criticism Reflection

- *Reflect on instances where you received constructive criticism and the subsequent improvements made.*
- *Seek out feedback from mentors, peers, or colleagues, actively using it as a tool for growth.*
- *Develop a mindset that sees feedback, even when challenging, as a catalyst for positive change.*

4. Celebrate Others' Success:

A growth mindset extends beyond individual accomplishments to the success of others. Instead of viewing others' achievements as threats, celebrate them as sources of inspiration and motivation. Embrace the idea that the success of peers and colleagues does not diminish your capabilities but serves as a testament to the boundless potential for growth within each individual.

Technique: Collective Success Mindset

- *Actively celebrate the achievements of others in your personal and professional circles.*
- *Engage in collaborative efforts that foster a collective mindset of success for the entire team or community.*
- *Cultivate a sense of unity and shared achievement, reinforcing the belief that success is not a finite resource.*

5. Persist in the Face of Setbacks:

Resilience, a core component of a growth mindset, manifests in the ability to persist in the face of setbacks. Instead of viewing setbacks as indications of personal inadequacy, recognize them as inherent aspects of the change process. Develop the mental fortitude to learn from setbacks, adjust strategies, and persevere with renewed determination toward your goals.

Technique: Setback Reflection and Adjustment

- *Reflect on past setbacks and the lessons learned from each experience.*
- *Develop a plan for adjusting strategies in response to setbacks, focusing on continuous improvement.*
- *Cultivate a mindset that views setbacks as temporary hurdles rather than insurmountable roadblocks.*

A Garden of Growth Mindset Flourishes

Cultivating a growth mindset is akin to tending to a garden of possibilities, where the seeds of resilience, effort, and openness to learning sprout and blossom. By embracing challenges, recognizing the value of effort, learning from criticism, celebrating collective success, and persisting in the face of setbacks, individuals nurture the conditions for a growth mindset to flourish. As we engage in the transformative journey toward a growth mindset, it is essential to understand that the process is iterative and ongoing. The techniques outlined here serve as guiding lights, illuminating the path toward a mindset that embraces continuous learning and development. Through intentional practice and a commitment to personal evolution, individuals unlock the potential to navigate the complexities

Harnessing the Power of Positive Thinking and Self-Belief: The Lighthouse of Personal Transformation

In the tapestry of personal transformation, the radiant threads of positive thinking and self-belief weave a narrative of empowerment, resilience, and the unwavering conviction that change is not only possible but inevitable. Chapter 8 delves into the profound exploration of harnessing the transformative potential within the realms of positive thinking and self-belief, recognizing them as potent catalysts that propel individuals toward their desired goals and aspirations.

The Essence of Positive Thinking: Illuminating the Path Ahead

Positive thinking is not merely a fleeting state of mind; it is a conscious choice to cultivate an optimistic and constructive perspective, even in the face of challenges. The power of positive thinking lies not in denying the existence of difficulties but in reframing them as opportunities for growth and learning. It is a mindset that radiates hope, resilience, and a proactive approach to navigating the intricacies of personal evolution.

Cultivating Optimism:

Positive thinking cultivates optimism, a lens through which individuals interpret experiences in a favorable light. Instead of fixating on the negative aspects of a situation, individuals with a positive mindset seek the silver lining, fostering a mental environment conducive to growth and self-improvement.

Fostering Resilience:

Resilience, the ability to bounce back from setbacks, is a natural byproduct of positive thinking. When faced with challenges, individuals anchored in a positive mindset view them as temporary hurdles rather than insurmountable obstacles. This resilience becomes a bedrock for navigating the ebb and flow of life with grace and determination.

Promoting Well-Being:

Positive thinking contributes to overall well-being by influencing emotional and mental states. It serves as a buffer against stress, anxiety, and negativity, creating space for a more balanced and harmonious inner experience. The ripple effect of well-being extends beyond the individual, impacting relationships, work, and the overall quality of life.

The Transformative Power of Self-Belief: A Journey Within

Self-belief, the unwavering trust in one's capabilities and potential, acts as the driving force behind personal transformation. It is the foundation upon which individuals build the courage to pursue their aspirations, overcome obstacles, and persist in the face of challenges. Harnessing the power of self-belief is not a passive endeavor; it is an active engagement with one's inner narrative, shaping it into a story of empowerment and possibility.

Building Confidence:

Self-belief is synonymous with confidence—an essential attribute for embarking on any transformative journey. Confidence emanates from a deep-seated belief in one's abilities and a positive assessment of personal worth. As individuals cultivate self-belief, they naturally radiate confidence, influencing their actions and interactions with the world.

Embracing Challenges:

A robust self-belief system empowers individuals to embrace challenges rather than shy away from them. Instead of succumbing to self-doubt in the face of difficulties, those grounded in self-belief perceive challenges as opportunities for growth. This courageous approach expands the boundaries of what is achievable and propels individuals toward new heights.

Fueling Persistence:

Self-belief is the fuel that sustains persistence—the dogged determination to persevere through setbacks and pursue long-term goals. When confronted with obstacles, individuals with a strong sense of self-belief view them as temporary roadblocks, confident in their ability to find alternative routes to success.

Techniques for Cultivating Positive Thinking: A Radiant Mindset

Practice Gratitude: Gratitude is a cornerstone of positive thinking. Cultivate a habit of acknowledging and appreciating the positive aspects of life, both big and small. Keeping a gratitude journal, where you regularly jot down things you are thankful for, creates a mindset attuned to abundance and appreciation.

Challenge Negative Thoughts: Actively challenge and reframe negative thoughts. When faced with self-doubt or pessimism, question the validity of those thoughts and seek alternative, more constructive perspectives. This practice disrupts the cycle of negative thinking and opens space for positive and empowering beliefs.

Surround Yourself with Positivity: Your environment plays a crucial role in shaping your mindset. Surround yourself with positive influences, whether it be through supportive relationships, uplifting media, or inspiring literature. Create a positive echo chamber that reinforces optimistic thinking and fosters a sense of possibility.

Visualization for Success: Engage in visualization exercises where you vividly imagine yourself achieving your goals. Visualization creates a mental blueprint for success, embedding positive images in your subconscious mind. This practice not only enhances self-belief but also provides a clear roadmap for your journey.

Techniques for Cultivating Self-Belief: The Anchor Within

Acknowledge Achievements: Take time to acknowledge and celebrate your achievements, no matter how small. Reflecting on past successes reinforces the belief in your capabilities and builds a reservoir of confidence. Regularly revisit your accomplishments to bolster self-belief during challenging times.

Set Realistic Goals: Establish realistic and achievable goals that align with your values and aspirations. Accomplishing these goals contributes to a sense of competence and reinforces the belief that you have the power to shape your destiny. Celebrate milestones along the way to sustain a positive momentum.

Affirmations for Self-Belief: Incorporate positive affirmations into your daily routine. Craft statements that affirm your abilities, worth, and potential for growth. Regularly repeat these affirmations with conviction, allowing them to permeate your subconscious mind and fortify the foundation of self-belief.

Seek Feedback and Learn: Actively seek feedback from trusted mentors, colleagues, or friends. Embrace constructive feedback as a valuable tool for growth, recognizing that it provides insights into areas for improvement. The ability to accept feedback and learn from experiences reinforces self-belief in the capacity for continuous development.

Radiant Pathways to Transformation

With positive thinking and self-belief, we discover radiant pathways to personal transformation. As positive thoughts illuminate the way forward, self-belief becomes the steadfast anchor within, grounding us in the conviction that our potential knows no bounds. Together, these potent forces propel us toward the zenith of personal evolution, where the tapestry of positive thinking and self-belief creates a masterpiece of resilience, optimism, and the unwavering belief in the transformative power within.

Part 3

The 30-Day Diary - A Journey Within

Welcome to the transformative heart of "Change Your Life in 30 Days: A Guide to Personal Transformation." In Part 3, we embark on a deeply personal odyssey—a 30-day diary that transcends the conventional boundaries of self-help literature. This section isn't just about absorbing information; it's about active engagement, introspection, and the conscious shaping of your daily experiences. Get ready to navigate the intricate landscape of your behavioural change with Chapter 9 as your compass, guiding you through the preparations for a journey that unfolds across Chapters 10-39, culminating in Chapter 40—a moment of profound reflection and celebration.

Chapter 9

Preparing for Your Transformation Journey

As you stand at the threshold of your 30-day diary, envision Chapter 9 as the vestibule—a space for preparation and anticipation. Here, we set the stage for your transformative journey, not just logistically, but mentally and emotionally. This chapter is a call to embrace the upcoming 30 days with intention, resilience, and a willingness to explore the depths of your own potential.

Setting the Stage for the 30-Day Diary

In this chapter, we lay the groundwork for your diary entries, emphasizing that this isn't a mere documentation of actions but a profound exploration of thoughts, emotions, and the essence of your being. Consider creating a dedicated space for your diary, a sanctuary where your reflections can unfold without inhibition. Embrace the anticipation of change as you make a conscious commitment to embark on this transformative journey.

Explore different approaches to journaling, whether it be a chronological account or a thematic reflection based on your evolving experiences. Prioritize authenticity in your entries, celebrating both victories and challenges as integral components of your growth story. Recognize your diary as a trusted confidant, ready to witness and support your innermost thoughts and experiences.

Reflect on the strength and resilience you've cultivated thus far, recognizing the inherent power within you. Approach the impending journey with an open heart, fostering a mindset that welcomes change as a gateway to new possibilities. Surround yourself with a supportive environment, be it through connections with fellow participants or sources of inspiration that uplift your spirit.

Chapters 10-39: Daily Entries for the 30-Day Diary

The soul of Part 3 unfolds through the pages of your daily entries—Chapters 10 through 39. These chapters are your canvas, waiting for the strokes of your reflections, gratitude, and intentional actions. Each chapter corresponds to a day in your transformative journey, offering prompts designed to guide your exploration and set the stage for meaningful change.

Prompts for Reflection, Gratitude, and Action:

- ❖ Daily, you'll engage in reflections, acknowledging both the challenges faced and the triumphs celebrated.
- ❖ Cultivate gratitude by recognizing and appreciating aspects of your life that bring joy and fulfillment.
- ❖ Take intentional actions aligned with your transformation goals, understanding that every step contributes to your evolving narrative.

Space for Personal Notes and Insights:

- ❖ Your diary isn't confined by prompts. Use the space to capture personal notes, spontaneous insights, and revelations that emerge during your daily journey.

- Embrace the fluidity of the diary, allowing it to evolve with you over the 30 days.

Chapter 40: Reflection and Celebration

As you approach the culmination of your 30-day journey, Chapter 40 serves as a portal for reflection and celebration—a bridge between the past and the transformed future.

Wrapping Up the 30-Day Transformation Journey:

- Reflect on the cumulative impact of your efforts, observing the subtle and profound transformations that have unfolded.
- Acknowledge the lessons learned, recognizing the wisdom gained through each day's experiences.
- Embrace the resilience and commitment that have brought you to this transformative juncture.
- Reflecting on Progress and Lessons Learned:
- Engage in a comprehensive reflection, exploring the patterns, shifts, and insights gleaned throughout the 30 days.
- Celebrate the milestones, both small and significant, that mark your journey of personal evolution.
- Investigate the connections between your initial intentions and the tangible outcomes that have materialized.
- Celebrating Achievements and Looking Ahead to a Transformed Future:
- Celebrate your achievements, embracing a sense of pride and gratitude for the journey undertaken.
- Visualize the transformed future that beckons, informed by the growth and insights gathered during this transformative journey.
- Embrace the possibilities that lie ahead, recognizing that the journey of personal transformation is an ongoing exploration.

An Invitation to Continued Growth

The concluding section of the book, beyond Chapter 40, will encapsulate key takeaways and offer encouragement for your continued growth and self-improvement. It is a reminder that your journey of behavioural change extends far beyond these 30 days—an ongoing expedition towards a life shaped by intention, resilience, and the enduring power of transformation.

Setting the Stage for the 30-Day Diary: A Prelude to Transformation

In the realm of personal development, the concept of a 30-day diary stands as a potent catalyst for change, a canvas upon which individuals can paint the strokes of their aspirations and navigate the terrain of their inner worlds. Setting the stage for this transformative journey requires more than the mere introduction of prompts and spaces for daily reflections; it calls for a deliberate and conscious preparation, akin to tuning an instrument before a symphony. As we delve into the significance of setting the stage for the 30-day diary, we explore the psychological underpinnings, the practical considerations, and the emotional resonance that transforms this diary from a mere tool to a companion in the expedition of self-discovery.

Creating a Dedicated Space for Reflection: The Sanctum Within

One of the foundational aspects of preparing for the 30-day diary is the establishment of a dedicated space for reflection. This isn't just about finding a quiet corner or a comfortable chair; it's about creating a sanctuary—a sanctum within which the transformative alchemy can unfold. The choice of this space is deeply personal and holds symbolic significance. It might be a cozy nook bathed in natural light, a favorite chair by the window, or a quiet corner adorned with elements that inspire tranquility.

The act of designating a specific space for the diary introduces a ritualistic element. It communicates to the subconscious mind that this is a sacred time, a moment set aside for introspection and self-exploration. In this space, the diary becomes more than just a collection of entries; it becomes a portal to the inner realms, a place where thoughts crystallize, emotions find expression, and aspirations take root. This intentional creation of a reflective space sets the tone for a mindful and purposeful engagement with the 30-day journey.

Embracing the Anticipation of Change: A Conscious Commitment

As individuals prepare to embark on the 30-day diary, an essential component is embracing the anticipation of change. This involves a conscious commitment—a mental and emotional readiness to engage with the transformative process that lies ahead. Anticipation, in this context, is not merely an acknowledgment of the upcoming days but an active engagement with the potential for growth and self-discovery.

Acknowledging the anticipation of change involves cultivating a mindset that is receptive to possibilities. It requires individuals to view the 30-day diary not as a mundane task but as a dynamic exploration—a journey into the uncharted territories of their own thoughts, behaviours, and aspirations. This anticipation serves as a motivational force, propelling individuals to approach each entry with curiosity, openness, and a genuine desire for personal evolution.

Establishing a Framework for Entries: From Chronology to Themes

The structure of the 30-day diary is pivotal in shaping the depth and breadth of the transformative experience. Individuals may choose to approach their entries in a chronological fashion, capturing the ebb and flow of each day. Alternatively, a thematic approach may be adopted, where entries revolve around specific aspects or areas of focus. The choice of framework is subjective and should align with the individual's preferred style of reflection.

A chronological approach often mirrors the natural rhythm of life, capturing the nuances of daily experiences as they unfold. This format provides a narrative flow, allowing individuals to trace the evolution of their thoughts and emotions over the course of the 30 days. On the other hand, a thematic approach allows for a more targeted exploration. Each entry becomes an opportunity to delve deeply into specific aspects of personal development, whether it be gratitude, self-awareness, or goal-setting. Regardless of the chosen framework, the act of establishing a structure for entries instills a sense of purpose and organization. It transforms the diary from a blank canvas into a guided journey, providing a roadmap for exploration and self-discovery. This deliberate structuring also enhances the cohesiveness of the overall narrative, creating a meaningful trajectory that aligns with the individual's intentions for transformation.

Prioritizing Authenticity in Documentation: Triumphs and Challenges Alike

At the core of the 30-day diary is the commitment to authenticity—a commitment to document not only the triumphs but also the challenges that punctuate the journey. Authenticity in documentation involves a willingness to embrace vulnerability and transparency, recognizing that true growth emerges from the honest acknowledgment of both success and struggle. Triumphs, however small, deserve celebration within the pages of the diary. Each accomplishment, no matter how seemingly insignificant, contributes to the mosaic of personal development. Celebrating successes instills a positive reinforcement loop, reinforcing the individual's belief in their capabilities and fortifying the motivation to continue striving for positive change.

Challenges, on the other hand, are not to be relegated to the sidelines. They are an integral part of the growth process, offering valuable insights and opportunities for learning. By documenting challenges, individuals engage in a form of self-reflection that goes beyond surface-level observations. They delve into the root causes, the emotional responses, and the strategies employed to navigate difficulties, fostering a deeper understanding of their own behavioural patterns. The commitment to authenticity in documentation transforms the 30-day diary into a dynamic narrative—a story that unfolds with genuineness and depth. It becomes a reflection not just of achievements but of the resilience, adaptability, and self-awareness cultivated through the journey.

Viewing the Diary as a Trusted Confidant: Witnessing Innermost Thoughts

The 30-day diary is more than a record-keeping tool; it is a trusted confidant—a non-judgmental space where individuals can lay bare their innermost thoughts, emotions, and aspirations. This perspective transforms the act of journaling from a mechanical task to a cathartic experience—a form of self-expression that transcends the limitations of verbal communication. The diary, in this context, becomes a witness to the inner dialogue of the individual. It patiently receives the outpourings of joy, frustration, hope, and self-discovery. By viewing the diary as a confidant, individuals cultivate a sense of intimacy with their own reflections. This relationship fosters a sense of security, encouraging individuals to explore their thoughts and emotions with a level of vulnerability that might be challenging in other contexts.

In this trusted confidant, individuals find solace, reflection, and a repository for their evolving narratives. The diary becomes a mirror that reflects not only the external events of each day but also the internal landscape—a mirror that, with each entry, unveils a clearer and more profound reflection of the self.

The Prelude to Personal Transformation

As you set the stage for the 30-day diary, you embark on a prelude to personal transformation. The intentional creation of a dedicated reflective space, the embracing of anticipation, the establishment of a framework for entries, the commitment to authenticity, and the viewing of the diary as a confidant collectively contribute to a transformative experience.

This setting of the stage is not a passive preparation but an active engagement with the journey within. It lays the foundation for self-discovery, growth, and the unfolding of personal narratives that resonate with authenticity. As individuals turn the first pages of their 30-day diary, they step onto a path that transcends mere documentation—it becomes a pathway to self-awareness, resilience, and the profound transformation of their inner landscapes. In the alchemy of these intentional preparations, the 30-day diary emerges as a powerful instrument—a blank canvas awaiting the vibrant hues of personal evolution.

Guidelines for Documenting Progress and Experiences: *Navigating the Tapestry of Transformation*

The 30-day diary is more than a mere collection of entries; it is a dynamic tapestry that captures the essence of personal transformation. As individuals embark on this journey, the guidelines for documenting progress and experiences become the compass that steers them through the labyrinth of self-discovery. These guidelines are not rigid rules but gentle suggestions, inviting individuals to explore the depths of their thoughts, emotions, and actions. In this exploration, they unravel the threads of their own narratives, weaving a story that mirrors the evolution of their inner selves.

Cultivating Authenticity in Expression: Honoring Triumphs and Challenges

At the core of documenting progress and experiences lies the principle of authenticity—a commitment to truthfully and openly express the highs and lows of the journey. Triumphs, no matter how modest, deserve recognition within the pages of the diary. Each small victory is a testament to resilience, determination, and the capacity for positive change. Celebrating these moments, individuals not only acknowledge their achievements but also cultivate a positive reinforcement loop that fuels motivation.

Challenges, on the other hand, are not to be shunned or downplayed. They are integral aspects of the growth process, providing valuable insights and opportunities for learning. Documenting challenges involves more than recounting difficulties; it's an invitation to delve into the emotional responses, the strategies employed to navigate obstacles, and the lessons extracted from adversity. Embracing challenges as part of the narrative fosters a holistic understanding of personal development and sets the stage for transformative insights.

Fostering Reflection Through Thoughtful Prompts: A Journey of Self-Exploration

Guidelines for documenting progress and experiences often incorporate thoughtful prompts designed to guide reflections. These prompts act as catalysts for deeper introspection, inviting individuals to explore facets of their thoughts and emotions that may remain undiscovered in the routine of daily life. They serve as gentle nudges, encouraging individuals to contemplate specific aspects of their experiences and gain a nuanced understanding of their inner landscapes.

Prompts for reflection may vary, encompassing themes such as gratitude, self-awareness, goal-setting, and emotional well-being. Each prompt is a doorway into a different chamber of self-exploration, offering individuals the opportunity to navigate the intricate terrain of their thoughts and emotions. Through these guided reflections, the diary becomes a reflective companion, facilitating a dialogue between the individual and their own inner world.

Embracing Openness to Change: A Fluid and Adaptive Approach

While guidelines provide structure, they also advocate for a fluid and adaptive approach to documenting progress and experiences. Transformation is a dynamic process, and as such, individuals are encouraged to embrace the ebb and flow of their own journeys. This openness to change involves an acceptance that plans and intentions may evolve, and that the diary is a living document that can adapt to the evolving needs of the individual.

Fluidity in documentation allows for spontaneity and creativity. It acknowledges that insights may emerge unexpectedly, and that the diary is a canvas for expressing these revelations in the moment. This adaptive approach empowers individuals to be responsive to their own growth, ensuring that the documentation process remains a genuine reflection of their evolving narratives.

Balancing Depth and Brevity: Crafting Meaningful Entries

Effective documentation strikes a delicate balance between depth and brevity. While the aim is to capture meaningful insights and experiences, the process should not become cumbersome or overwhelming. Guidelines encourage individuals to distill their thoughts into concise yet impactful entries, focusing on the essence of their reflections.

Crafting meaningful entries involves the art of selecting key moments, insights, or emotional shifts that encapsulate the day's experience. This intentional selection not only streamlines the documentation process but also hones the skill of recognizing the core elements that contribute to personal growth. By striking this balance, individuals ensure that each entry becomes a poignant snapshot of their transformative journey.

Acknowledging Progress, Big and Small: Nurturing a Growth Mindset

Guidelines for documenting progress emphasize the importance of acknowledging progress, whether it's a monumental achievement or a small step forward. Nurturing a growth mindset involves recognizing that personal development is a journey of continuous improvement, and every positive action contributes to this evolution. Documenting even the seemingly minor victories cultivates a mindset that values progress over perfection.

Acknowledging progress, big and small, serves as a motivational tool. It reinforces the individual's belief in their capacity for positive change and encourages a forward momentum. Whether it's overcoming a significant challenge or consistently practicing a new habit, each acknowledgment becomes a building block in the construction of a growth-oriented mindset.

Infusing Creativity into Expression: Beyond Words on Paper

The act of documenting progress and experiences transcends the written word; it is an opportunity to infuse creativity into expression. Guidelines often encourage individuals to explore diverse forms of expression, from sketches and diagrams to collages and photographs. This creative dimension adds a visceral layer to the documentation process, allowing individuals to communicate their experiences in ways that extend beyond the constraints of language.

Infusing creativity into expression taps into different modes of cognition and self-reflection. Visual elements can capture emotions, symbolic representations, and the atmosphere of a particular moment in ways that words may fall short. This multi-sensory approach enhances the richness of the documentation, transforming the diary into a multi-dimensional reflection of the transformative journey.

Sharing Insights and Seeking Support: A Community of Growth

While the 30-day diary is a deeply personal endeavor, guidelines often suggest the potential benefits of sharing insights and seeking support. This communal aspect creates a network of growth—a community where individuals can exchange experiences, offer encouragement, and gain valuable perspectives. Sharing insights with trusted friends, family, or an online community fosters a sense of accountability and provides additional layers of support throughout the journey.

The act of articulating experiences to others reinforces personal insights and offers an external perspective that may illuminate blind spots. Additionally, receiving support and encouragement from a community creates a synergistic effect, amplifying the motivation and sense of shared purpose among individuals pursuing their own paths of transformation.

A Dynamic Canvas of Personal Evolution

As you adhere to the guidelines for documenting progress and experiences within the 30-day diary, you embark on a dynamic journey of personal evolution. This documentation process is not a mechanical task but a living, breathing expression of the transformative journey. It is a canvas upon which you weave the threads of your experiences, challenges, triumphs, and reflections, creating a tapestry that mirrors the intricate beauty of your own growth. In adhering to these guidelines, the diary becomes more than a record—it becomes a testament to the resilience, self-discovery, and the unwavering commitment to *your* personal transformation.

Cultivating a Supportive Mindset for the Journey Ahead: Nurturing the Seeds of Transformation

As individuals embark on the transformative odyssey of a 30-day diary, the significance of cultivating a supportive mindset cannot be overstated. This mindset acts as the fertile soil in which the seeds of personal growth are sown, nurtured, and ultimately blossom into profound transformations. The journey ahead is not merely a collection of days; it is an exploration of self, a narrative of resilience, and a testament to the power of intentional change. In cultivating a supportive mindset, individuals lay the foundation for a journey marked by self-compassion, resilience, and an unwavering commitment to personal evolution.

Embracing Self-Compassion as a Cornerstone: A Gentle Embrace

At the heart of cultivating a supportive mindset lies the cornerstone of self-compassion. This involves extending to oneself the same kindness, understanding, and encouragement that one might readily offer to a friend facing challenges. The 30-day diary is not a battleground for self-criticism; it is a sacred space for growth, exploration, and the acknowledgment of one's humanity.

Self-compassion allows individuals to approach the journey with a gentleness that recognizes the inevitability of setbacks and the fluctuations inherent in the process of change. It is an invitation to let go of the harsh inner critic and, instead, adopt an attitude of self-kindness. As individuals encounter hurdles or moments of vulnerability, self-compassion becomes the balm that soothes the wounds, fostering an environment of emotional safety that is conducive to meaningful exploration and transformation.

Cultivating a Growth Mindset: Embracing Challenges as Opportunities

A supportive mindset is intrinsically tied to the cultivation of a growth mindset—a belief that challenges, setbacks, and even failures are not roadblocks but opportunities for learning and development. Individuals with a growth mindset perceive their abilities and intelligence as malleable, understanding that effort and resilience are key contributors to personal evolution.

In the context of the 30-day diary, cultivating a growth mindset involves reframing challenges as integral components of the transformative journey. Instead of viewing difficulties as insurmountable obstacles, individuals with a growth mindset approach them with curiosity, seeking the lessons embedded within the challenges. This mindset shift not only propels individuals forward in the face of adversity but also fosters a sense of empowerment, as each challenge becomes a stepping stone toward greater self-awareness and resilience.

Affirming Positive Intentions: Crafting an Empowering Narrative

A supportive mindset is rooted in the affirmations of positive intentions—an intentional crafting of an empowering narrative that aligns with the individual's vision for personal growth. Affirmations serve as guiding lights, illuminating the path ahead and reinforcing a positive and constructive self-perception. As individuals document their experiences in the 30-day diary, affirmations become the scaffolding upon which a transformative narrative is built.

Affirmations need not be grandiose; they can be simple yet potent statements that reflect the individual's aspirations, values, and commitment to change. Whether affirming resilience in the face of challenges, acknowledging the capacity for growth, or expressing gratitude for the journey itself, these positive intentions contribute to the creation of a mental framework that empowers individuals to navigate the twists and turns of their transformative expedition.

Cultivating Resilience: The Art of Bouncing Back

Resilience is the cornerstone of a supportive mindset, embodying the art of bouncing back from setbacks and challenges. The 30-day diary is not a linear progression; it is a dynamic journey marked by peaks and valleys. Cultivating resilience involves recognizing that setbacks are not indicative of failure but are, in fact, integral components of the growth process.

Individuals with a resilient mindset view challenges as opportunities for adaptation and growth. Rather than succumbing to discouragement, they bounce back with renewed determination, armed with the lessons gleaned from adversity. The cultivation of resilience is a conscious choice to face challenges with courage, embracing the inherent unpredictability of the transformative journey and using each experience as a stepping stone toward personal evolution.

Building a Supportive Environment: Connecting with Resources

Cultivating a supportive mindset extends beyond individual introspection; it encompasses the creation of an external environment that nurtures personal growth. This involves identifying and connecting with resources that offer inspiration, guidance, and a sense of community. Supportive environments can take various forms, from engaging with like-minded individuals in person or online to seeking guidance from mentors, books, or other sources of inspiration.

Building a supportive environment is an active and intentional process. It involves curating a space that fosters positivity, growth, and a sense of belonging. Whether through joining a community of individuals on similar journeys, participating in discussions, or immersing oneself in literature that resonates with personal values, the external environment becomes a mirror of the internal mindset, amplifying the individual's commitment to transformation.

Practicing Mindfulness: Anchoring in the Present Moment

A supportive mindset is anchored in mindfulness—a practice that involves being fully present and engaged in the current moment. The 30-day diary is not just about the destination; it is about the journey, the process, and the unfolding of each day. Mindfulness allows individuals to appreciate the nuances of their experiences, fostering a deeper connection with their thoughts, emotions, and actions.

Mindfulness involves cultivating an awareness of the present moment without judgment. It encourages individuals to observe their thoughts and feelings with curiosity, allowing for a non-reactive and intentional engagement with the unfolding journey. By anchoring in the present moment, individuals with a supportive mindset create a foundation for meaningful self-discovery and growth.

Balancing Reflection with Action: A Dynamic Interplay

A supportive mindset is characterized by a dynamic interplay between reflection and action. While reflection provides the space for introspection and self-awareness, action propels individuals forward on their transformative journey. The 30-day diary is a tool for both contemplation and intentional action, and a supportive mindset strikes a balance between the two.

Reflection without action may result in stagnation, while action without reflection may lead to aimless motion. Cultivating a supportive mindset involves recognizing the symbiotic relationship between contemplation and intentional steps toward personal goals. This dynamic interplay ensures that each entry in the diary is not merely a record but a catalyst for purposeful and transformative action.

Nurturing the Seeds of Transformation

In the cultivation of a supportive mindset for the journey ahead, individuals embark on a profound exploration of self-discovery and growth. This mindset becomes the nurturing soil in which the seeds of transformation are planted, taking root and flourishing over the course of the 30-day diary. As individuals navigate the peaks and valleys of their transformative journey, a supportive mindset serves as the compass, guiding them with compassion, resilience, and an unwavering commitment to personal evolution. It is not just a mindset; it is a sanctuary—a nurturing space that fosters the flourishing of the individual on their path of self-discovery and positive change.

Chapter 10-39

Embarking on the Daily Journey: A Preview of Chapters 10-39

As we delve into Chapters 10-39 of the 30-day diary, we step into the heart of the transformative journey. Each chapter unfolds as a canvas, capturing the essence of a single day in the pursuit of personal growth. This section of the book is designed to be your companion, offering daily prompts for reflection, gratitude, and action. It provides a sacred space for personal notes and insights, serving as a reservoir for the thoughts and emotions that surface throughout your transformative expedition.

Within these chapters, expect a carefully curated blend of introspection and intentional action. Each day brings forth a unique opportunity to explore the depths of self-awareness, express gratitude for the present moment, and take deliberate steps toward positive change. The prompts provided are not rigid directives but gentle invitations, encouraging you to navigate the landscape of your thoughts and emotions with curiosity and openness.

As you progress through Chapters 10-39, envision this section as a dynamic map guiding you through the intricate terrain of your own transformation. It's not just a record of days passed; it's an interactive experience, a dialogue between you and the unfolding narrative of your growth. So, fasten your seatbelt and prepare to immerse yourself in the daily rhythm of reflection, gratitude, and action—unveiling new layers of self-discovery with each turn of the page.

These prompts are designed to encourage introspection, foster gratitude, and inspire intentional action throughout your 30-day transformation process. Feel free to adapt them to your personal preferences and circumstances.

Reflect on a recent behaviour or decision that brought positive outcomes. What can you learn from this experience?

Day 1:

Start by writing your Change Statement as though you have already transformed yourself.

Today, I realised my profound transformation and I am now...

On a scale of 1 - 10 with one being zero motivation and 10 being Supercharged Motivation, where is your motivation to realise your change ambition?

Why did I choose this figure?

What can motivate me more today?
_____
_____
_____

How did I do today and what steps will I take tomorrow to succeed?
_____
_____
_____

Practice Gratitude: List three things you are grateful for in your current environment.

Day 2:

Start by writing your Change Statement as though you have already transformed yourself.

Today, I realised my profound transformation and I am now...

On a scale of 1 - 10 with one being zero motivation and 10 being Supercharged Motivation, where is your motivation to realise your change ambition?

Why did I choose this figure?

What can motivate me more today?
___

___

___

How did I do today and what steps will I take tomorrow to succeed?
___

___

___

Take Action: Set a clear intention for the day ahead. What positive action can you take to align with this intention?

Day 3:

Start by writing your Change Statement as though you have already transformed yourself.

Today, I realised my profound transformation and I am now…

On a scale of 1 - 10 with one being zero motivation and 10 being Supercharged Motivation, where is your motivation to realise your change ambition?

Why did I choose this figure?

What can motivate me more today?
_____
_____
_____
_____

How did I do today and what steps will I take tomorrow to succeed?
_____
_____

Reflection: Dive into a challenging moment from your past. How did you handle it, and what insights can you gain for future resilience?

Day 4:

Start by writing your Change Statement as though you have already transformed yourself.

Today, I realised my profound transformation and I am now…

On a scale of 1 - 10 with one being zero motivation and 10 being Supercharged Motivation, where is your motivation to realise your change ambition?

Why did I choose this figure?

What can motivate me more today?

How did I do today and what steps will I take tomorrow to succeed?

Practice Gratitude: Express gratitude for a supportive person in your life and consider ways to show your appreciation.

Day 5:

Start by writing your Change Statement as though you have already transformed yourself.

Today, I realised my profound transformation and I am now...

On a scale of 1 - 10 with one being zero motivation and 10 being Supercharged Motivation, where is your motivation to realise your change ambition?

Why did I choose this figure?

What can motivate me more today?
___

___

___

How did I do today and what steps will I take tomorrow to succeed?
___

___

Take Action: Identify a habit you want to cultivate. Outline specific steps to incorporate it into your routine.

Day 6:

Start by writing your Change Statement as though you have already transformed yourself.

Today, I realised my profound transformation and I am now...

On a scale of 1 - 10 with one being zero motivation and 10 being Supercharged Motivation, where is your motivation to realise your change ambition?

Why did I choose this figure?

What can motivate me more today?
___

___

___

How did I do today and what steps will I take tomorrow to succeed?
___

___

Reflection: Reflect on a personal quality or skill you possess. How has it contributed to your well-being?

Day 7:

Start by writing your Change Statement as though you have already transformed yourself.

Today, I realised my profound transformation and I am now...

On a scale of 1 - 10 with one being zero motivation and 10 being Supercharged Motivation, where is your motivation to realise your change ambition?

Why did I choose this figure?

What can motivate me more today?

How did I do today and what steps will I take tomorrow to succeed?

Practice Gratitude: Appreciate a challenging experience for the lessons it brought. What silver lining can you find?

Day 8:

Start by writing your Change Statement as though you have already transformed yourself.

Today, I realised my profound transformation and I am now...

On a scale of 1 - 10 with one being zero motivation and 10 being Supercharged Motivation, where is your motivation to realise your change ambition?

Why did I choose this figure?

What can motivate me more today?
_____
_____
_____

How did I do today and what steps will I take tomorrow to succeed?
_____
_____

***Take Action:** Reach out to someone you haven't connected with in a while. Share a positive experience or express your gratitude.*

Day 9:

Start by writing your Change Statement as though you have already transformed yourself.

Today, I realised my profound transformation and I am now...

On a scale of 1 - 10 with one being zero motivation and 10 being Supercharged Motivation, where is your motivation to realise your change ambition?

Why did I choose this figure?

What can motivate me more today?

How did I do today and what steps will I take tomorrow to succeed?

Reflect: Consider a recent challenge. What were your initial thoughts and emotions, and how did they evolve?

Day 10:

Start by writing your Change Statement as though you have already transformed yourself.

Today, I realised my profound transformation and I am now...

On a scale of 1 - 10 with one being zero motivation and 10 being Supercharged Motivation, where is your motivation to realise your change ambition?

Why did I choose this figure?

What can motivate me more today?

How did I do today and what steps will I take tomorrow to succeed?

Practice Gratitude: Take a moment to express gratitude for your body and its ability to support you every day.

Day 11:

Start by writing your Change Statement as though you have already transformed yourself.

Today, I realised my profound transformation and I am now...

On a scale of 1 - 10 with one being zero motivation and 10 being Supercharged Motivation, where is your motivation to realise your change ambition?

Why did I choose this figure?

What can motivate me more today?
___

___

___

How did I do today and what steps will I take tomorrow to succeed?
___

___

Take Action: Choose a fear or obstacle you've been avoiding. Develop a small, actionable step to confront or overcome it.

Day 12:

Start by writing your Change Statement as though you have already transformed yourself.

Today, I realised my profound transformation and I am now...

On a scale of 1 - 10 with one being zero motivation and 10 being Supercharged Motivation, where is your motivation to realise your change ambition?

Why did I choose this figure?

What can motivate me more today?
_____
_____
_____
_____

How did I do today and what steps will I take tomorrow to succeed?
_____
_____

Reflect: Reflect on a significant life event. How has it shaped your current beliefs and values?

Day 13:

Start by writing your Change Statement as though you have already transformed yourself.

Today, I realised my profound transformation and I am now…

On a scale of 1 - 10 with one being zero motivation and 10 being Supercharged Motivation, where is your motivation to realise your change ambition?

Why did I choose this figure?

What can motivate me more today?
___

___

___

How did I do today and what steps will I take tomorrow to succeed?
___

___

Practice Gratitude: List three qualities you appreciate about yourself.

Day 14:

Start by writing your Change Statement as though you have already transformed yourself.

Today, I realised my profound transformation and I am now…

On a scale of 1 - 10 with one being zero motivation and 10 being Supercharged Motivation, where is your motivation to realise your change ambition?

Why did I choose this figure?

What can motivate me more today?
_____
_____
_____
_____

How did I do today and what steps will I take tomorrow to succeed?
_____
_____
_____

Take Action: Set a goal for personal growth. What actionable steps can you take to work toward this goal?

Day 15:

Start by writing your Change Statement as though you have already transformed yourself.

Today, I realised my profound transformation and I am now…

On a scale of 1 - 10 with one being zero motivation and 10 being Supercharged Motivation, where is your motivation to realise your change ambition?

Why did I choose this figure?

What can motivate me more today?
_____
_____
_____
_____

How did I do today and what steps will I take tomorrow to succeed?
_____
_____

Reflect: Dive into a challenging moment from your past. How did you handle it, and what insights can you gain for future resilience?

Day 16:

Start by writing your Change Statement as though you have already transformed yourself.

Today, I realised my profound transformation and I am now...

On a scale of 1 - 10 with one being zero motivation and 10 being Supercharged Motivation, where is your motivation to realise your change ambition?

Why did I choose this figure?

What can motivate me more today?

How did I do today and what steps will I take tomorrow to succeed?

Practice Gratitude: Express gratitude for the support systems in your life—friends, family, or colleagues.

Day 17:

Start by writing your Change Statement as though you have already transformed yourself.

Today, I realised my profound transformation and I am now...

On a scale of 1 - 10 with one being zero motivation and 10 being Supercharged Motivation, where is your motivation to realise your change ambition?

Why did I choose this figure?

What can motivate me more today?
_____
_____
_____

How did I do today and what steps will I take tomorrow to succeed?
_____
_____

Take Action: Commit to a random act of kindness today. How can you make a positive impact on someone else's day?

Day 18:

Start by writing your Change Statement as though you have already transformed yourself.

Today, I realised my profound transformation and I am now…

On a scale of 1 - 10 with one being zero motivation and 10 being Supercharged Motivation, where is your motivation to realise your change ambition?

Why did I choose this figure?

What can motivate me more today?

How did I do today and what steps will I take tomorrow to succeed?

Reflect: Explore the concept of identity. How does your self-perception influence your decision-making?

Day 19:

Start by writing your Change Statement as though you have already transformed yourself.

Today, I realised my profound transformation and I am now...

On a scale of 1 - 10 with one being zero motivation and 10 being Supercharged Motivation, where is your motivation to realise your change ambition?

Why did I choose this figure?

What can motivate me more today?
___

___

___

How did I do today and what steps will I take tomorrow to succeed?
___

___

Practice Gratitude: Reflect on a valuable lesson from a past mistake. What growth has it facilitated?

Day 20:

Start by writing your Change Statement as though you have already transformed yourself.

Today, I realised my profound transformation and I am now...

On a scale of 1 - 10 with one being zero motivation and 10 being Supercharged Motivation, where is your motivation to realise your change ambition?

Why did I choose this figure?

What can motivate me more today?
___

___

___

How did I do today and what steps will I take tomorrow to succeed?
___

___

Take Action: Volunteer or contribute to a cause you believe in. How can your actions make a positive difference?

Day 21:

Start by writing your Change Statement as though you have already transformed yourself.

Today, I realised my profound transformation and I am now...

On a scale of 1 - 10 with one being zero motivation and 10 being Supercharged Motivation, where is your motivation to realise your change ambition?

Why did I choose this figure?

What can motivate me more today?
_____
_____
_____

How did I do today and what steps will I take tomorrow to succeed?
_____
_____

***Reflect:** Contemplate a decision you regret. What lessons can you extract from this experience?*

Day 22:

Start by writing your Change Statement as though you have already transformed yourself.

Today, I realised my profound transformation and I am now…

On a scale of 1 - 10 with one being zero motivation and 10 being Supercharged Motivation, where is your motivation to realise your change ambition?

Why did I choose this figure?

What can motivate me more today?

How did I do today and what steps will I take tomorrow to succeed?

Practice Gratitude: Appreciate a skill or talent you possess. How can you further develop and utilize it?

Day 23:

Start by writing your Change Statement as though you have already transformed yourself.

Today, I realised my profound transformation and I am now…

On a scale of 1 - 10 with one being zero motivation and 10 being Supercharged Motivation, where is your motivation to realise your change ambition?

Why did I choose this figure?

What can motivate me more today?
_____
_____
_____

How did I do today and what steps will I take tomorrow to succeed?
_____
_____

Take Action: Practice a form of self-care that aligns with your well-being. How can you prioritize self-nurturing today?

Day 24:

Start by writing your Change Statement as though you have already transformed yourself.

Today, I realised my profound transformation and I am now...

On a scale of 1 - 10 with one being zero motivation and 10 being Supercharged Motivation, where is your motivation to realise your change ambition?

Why did I choose this figure?

What can motivate me more today?
_____
_____
_____
_____

How did I do today and what steps will I take tomorrow to succeed?
_____
_____

Reflect: Reflect on a current struggle. How might reframing your perspective offer new insights?

Day 25:

Start by writing your Change Statement as though you have already transformed yourself.

Today, I realised my profound transformation and I am now...

On a scale of 1 - 10 with one being zero motivation and 10 being Supercharged Motivation, where is your motivation to realise your change ambition?

Why did I choose this figure?

What can motivate me more today?
___

___

___

___

How did I do today and what steps will I take tomorrow to succeed?
___

___

Practice Gratitude: Acknowledge the positive impact of nature on your well-being. Express gratitude for the natural elements around you.

Day 26:

Start by writing your Change Statement as though you have already transformed yourself.

Today, I realised my profound transformation and I am now...

On a scale of 1 - 10 with one being zero motivation and 10 being Supercharged Motivation, where is your motivation to realise your change ambition?

Why did I choose this figure?

What can motivate me more today?

How did I do today and what steps will I take tomorrow to succeed?

Take Action: Identify a negative thought pattern. Develop a strategy to replace it with a more positive perspective.

Day 27:

Start by writing your Change Statement as though you have already transformed yourself.

Today, I realised my profound transformation and I am now...

On a scale of 1 - 10 with one being zero motivation and 10 being Supercharged Motivation, where is your motivation to realise your change ambition?

Why did I choose this figure?

What can motivate me more today?
_____
_____
_____

How did I do today and what steps will I take tomorrow to succeed?
_____
_____

Reflect: Explore a recurring pattern in your behaviour. What steps can you take to break this pattern and foster positive change?

Day 28:

Start by writing your Change Statement as though you have already transformed yourself.

Today, I realised my profound transformation and I am now...

On a scale of 1 - 10 with one being zero motivation and 10 being Supercharged Motivation, where is your motivation to realise your change ambition?

Why did I choose this figure?

What can motivate me more today?

How did I do today and what steps will I take tomorrow to succeed?

Practice Gratitude: In the face of recent challenges, express gratitude for the transformative lessons they brought, recognizing them as catalysts for growth and resilience.

Day 29:

Start by writing your Change Statement as though you have already transformed yourself.

Today, I realised my profound transformation and I am now…

On a scale of 1 - 10 with one being zero motivation and 10 being Supercharged Motivation, where is your motivation to realise your change ambition?

Why did I choose this figure?

What can motivate me more today?

How did I do today and what steps will I take tomorrow to succeed?

Take Action: Share your transformation journey with someone you trust. How can their support enhance your experience?

Day 30:

Start by writing your Change Statement as though you have already transformed yourself.

Today, I realised my profound transformation and I am now...

On a scale of 1 - 10 with one being zero motivation and 10 being Supercharged Motivation, where is your motivation to realise your change ambition?

Why did I choose this figure?

What can motivate me more today?
_____
_____
_____

How did I do today and what steps will I take tomorrow to succeed?
_____

Chapter 40

Embracing Transformation: A Prelude to Chapter 40

As we stand at the threshold of Chapter 40, we find ourselves at the culmination of a remarkable journey—a 30-day odyssey of self-discovery, growth, and intentional change. This chapter serves as a poignant reflection and celebration, inviting you to cast a retrospective gaze on the path you've traversed and the milestones you've achieved.

In the spirit of reflection, this chapter encourages you to delve into the nuances of your progress and glean lessons from the experiences that have shaped your transformation. It beckons you to unravel the layers of self-awareness cultivated throughout the journey, acknowledging the triumphs and challenges that have sculpted your evolving narrative.

Celebration becomes the heartbeat of Chapter 40—an acknowledgment of the resilience, commitment, and positive change that has unfolded over the past 30 days. It's a moment to revel in the victories, both grand and subtle, that have punctuated your transformative expedition. The celebration is not merely an external affirmation but an internal recognition of your capacity for growth and the intentional steps taken toward a more empowered and authentic self.

As you turn the pages of Chapter 40, envision it as a sacred space for reflection, gratitude, and jubilation—a space to bid farewell to the past 30 days with a sense of accomplishment and to embrace the promise of a transformed future. It marks not an end but a transition—an entryway to continued growth, self-improvement, and the limitless possibilities that await on the horizon. So, let the celebration commence as we wrap up this transformative journey with hearts full of gratitude and eyes fixed on the transformative potential that lies ahead.

Wrapping Up the 30-Day Transformation Journey: A Tapestry of Growth

As we approach the conclusion of this transformative expedition, take a moment to breathe in the essence of the 30-day journey—a journey marked by self-discovery, intentional change, and a commitment to personal growth. Wrapping up this transformative chapter is not merely a conclusion; it's a pause, a reflective interlude where you stand at the intersection of your past and the vast potential of your future.

The culmination of the 30-day transformation journey invites you to gather the threads of experiences, insights, and challenges encountered along the way. Like an intricately woven tapestry, each day has contributed a unique hue, creating a mosaic that reflects the richness of your commitment to change. It's a moment to acknowledge the resilience that carried you through moments of doubt, the curiosity that fueled introspection, and the willingness to embrace the discomfort that accompanies growth.

Reflect on the patterns that have emerged, recognizing the subtle shifts in mindset, habits, and perspectives. This reflective process is not about scrutinizing for perfection but celebrating the imperfect, acknowledging the beauty in the journey's ebb and flow. As you wrap up this transformative chapter, envision the 30 days as a foundation—a solid ground upon which you've built a framework for sustained personal development.

This concluding moment serves as a bridge to what lies beyond—a future brimming with potential and untapped possibilities. The 30-day journey may be concluding, but the transformative ripple effect it has initiated within you continues to echo into the future. As you wrap up this chapter, carry forward the lessons learned, the strengths discovered, and the growth achieved, for they will be the compass guiding you toward a future shaped by intentional choices, self-awareness, and a continued commitment to personal evolution.

Reflecting on Progress and Lessons Learned: The Mirrors of Transformation

In the quiet moments of reflection that punctuate the conclusion of this 30-day journey, it's time to gaze into the mirrors of progress and lessons learned. Reflecting on the path traversed unveils a tapestry of growth woven with the threads of self-awareness, resilience, and intentional change.

Take a moment to acknowledge the milestones achieved—a collection of small victories and significant breakthroughs that have marked your progression. Reflect on the habits cultivated, the mindsets shifted, and the awareness deepened. Celebrate the courage that propelled you forward during challenging times and the commitment that sustained your journey.

Equally vital is the exploration of lessons learned. Reflection is not merely about celebrating successes; it's an excavation process, unearthing the buried gems of insight from setbacks and challenges. Consider the moments that tested your resolve, the obstacles that shaped your resilience, and the unexpected lessons that transformed perceived failures into stepping stones for growth.

Reflecting on progress and lessons learned is an exercise in self-compassion—a recognition that growth is a dynamic process with its ebbs and flows. Embrace the imperfections, for within them lies the raw material for authentic transformation. As you navigate the landscape of reflection, distill the essence of your experiences into wisdom, an invaluable compass guiding future decisions and actions.

This reflective interlude is a bridge between the past and the unwritten chapters of your future. It's an acknowledgment that every step, whether forward or stumbled upon, has contributed to the evolving narrative of your journey. So, as you ponder the mirrors reflecting your progress and lessons learned, carry forward the insights gained, allowing them to illuminate the path that stretches ahead—an open canvas waiting for the brushstrokes of your continued growth.

Celebrating Achievements and Embracing a Transformed Future: A Symphony of Triumph

In the grand finale of this 30-day metamorphosis, let the jubilation resound as you celebrate the achievements scattered along the trail of intentional change. Each milestone, no matter how modest, is a note in the symphony of triumph—a melody that harmonizes with the rhythm of your commitment to growth.

Take stock of the victories, both overt and subtle, that have embellished your transformative journey. Celebrate the habits cultivated, the patterns disrupted, and the resilience forged in the crucible of challenges. Acknowledge the dedication that fueled your progress and the newfound self-awareness that illuminated your path. Each triumph, a testament to your unwavering commitment to a better, more authentic version of yourself.

As you revel in the accomplishments, cast your gaze forward, for this celebration is not merely an endpoint but a gateway to a transformed future. Envision the person you have become—the one who navigated the terrain of change with courage and embraced the discomfort as a herald of growth. This celebration is a recognition that you are not the same person who embarked on this journey—a metamorphosis, a rebirth, a phoenix rising from the ashes of old paradigms.

Looking ahead, anticipate a future shaped by intentional choices and empowered decisions. The achievements celebrated today are not fleeting moments but stepping stones toward sustained growth. Embrace the promise of a transformed future, where the lessons learned and victories attained pave the way for continued evolution. As you stand at this crossroads, let the celebration echo into the horizon, propelling you forward with the knowledge that your journey is an ever-unfolding narrative—a story of triumph, resilience, and the limitless potential of the transformed self.

Nurturing the Seeds of Change

As we draw the curtains on this transformative journey, it is a moment to gather the threads of insight and growth woven through the chapters of "Change Your Life in 30 Days: A Guide to Personal Transformation." This book has been a companion on your expedition into the realms of self-awareness, intentional change, and the profound power of behavioural transformation. Let's recap the key takeaways that have marked this odyssey of personal development.

Conclusion

Recap of Key Takeaways:

In the exploration of behavioural patterns, we unveiled the intricate tapestry of our habits, triggers, and the influence of our past experiences. Identifying psychological triggers, understanding the impact of childhood on our perception, and recognizing the connection between identity and decision-making became waypoints on the map to self-discovery.

Strategies and tools for behavioural change equipped us with the tools needed for lasting transformation. From setting powerful intentions and building new habits to managing resistance and cultivating a growth mindset, each chapter provided actionable steps toward positive change.

The 30-day diary, a reflective journaling journey, served as a personalized roadmap for daily introspection, gratitude, and intentional action. It became the canvas upon which the story of your transformation unfolded, fostering a supportive mindset for your evolution.

Encouragement for Continued Growth:

As we stand at the threshold of this conclusion, let the echoes of encouragement resonate within. Your journey doesn't conclude with the turning of these pages; it extends into the uncharted territories of your future. Embrace the spirit of continuous growth and self-improvement. Understand that each day is a new canvas, an opportunity to paint the strokes of intentional change.

Final Thoughts on the Power of behavioural Change:

The power of behavioural change is not a singular moment but a continuous, evolving force. It's a ripple effect that extends beyond the individual, touching the lives of those around you and creating a positive impact on the world. As you navigate the complexities of life, remember that your capacity for change is boundless.

In conclusion, this book is not a final destination but a compass pointing toward a future imbued with the promise of transformation. Nurture the seeds of change you've planted, water them with intention, and watch as they blossom into a life rich with authenticity, purpose, and fulfillment. The journey doesn't end here; it unfolds with every choice you make, every lesson you learn, and every intentional step you take toward becoming the best version of yourself. May your path be illuminated by the enduring light of personal growth and the unwavering belief in the transformative power within you.

Printed in France by Amazon
Brétigny-sur-Orge, FR